William John Charles Moens

English Travellers and Italian Brigands

A Narrative of Capture and Captivity

William John Charles Moens

English Travellers and Italian Brigands
A Narrative of Capture and Captivity

ISBN/EAN: 9783741112539

Manufactured in Europe, USA, Canada, Australia, Japa

Cover: Foto ©Andreas Hilbeck / pixelio.de

Manufactured and distributed by brebook publishing software (www.brebook.com)

William John Charles Moens

English Travellers and Italian Brigands

ENGLISH TRAVELLERS

AND

ITALIAN BRIGANDS.

A NARRATIVE OF CAPTURE AND CAPTIVITY.

BY

W. J. C. MOENS.

CAPITANO MANZO.

IN TWO VOLS.—VOL. I.

LONDON:
HURST AND BLACKETT, PUBLISHERS,
13, GREAT MARLBOROUGH STREET.
1866.

The right of Translation is reserved.

PREFACE.

The great interest manifested in the misfortune with which the Reverend J. C. Murray Aynsley and I met during our visit to Southern Italy in the spring of this year (coupled with the request of many of my friends that I should publish some account of my experiences there), induces me to hope that a description of my adventures in the mountains near Salerno may not be unacceptable to my countrymen, particularly as little is known in England of the "domestic" life of Italian brigands, very few (if indeed any) Englishmen having had such an opportunity of observing brigand manners as has fallen to my lot. And I sincerely trust it may be long before any of my countrymen has the misfortune to become so intimately acquainted, as I have become, with the mode of life followed by these free companions.*

The book which I venture to offer to the public has no pretensions whatever to literary merit of any sort. I have endeavoured to describe, as simply as possible, what took place from day to day during my captivity, and I trust that the many shortcomings of the work may be considered as atoned for in some degree by the novelty of at all events some part of what I have attempted to describe.

To make the narrative complete, my wife has supplied from her diary an account of what my friends were doing for me outside my prison; and we have prefixed three chapters recounting our visit to Sicily, which, as having taken place

* Since my release, it has been announced that five other persons have been taken by my captors—none of them, however, Englishmen.

PREFACE. vii

at the time Mount Etna was in active eruption, and also as having introduced us to Sicilian brigands, I hope may not be entirely without interest.

I have also ventured to add a few general remarks on Neapolitan brigandage, and the only cures which my experience enables me to suggest for it. If the truth has obliged me to make any remarks on this subject, which put the state of brigandage under the present Government in somewhat unfavourable contrast with what it was under the Bourbons, it must not be thought on that account that I am at all inclined to favour the latter. From the bottom of my heart I wish well to United Italy; but for all that, while fully appreciating the difficulties of the new Government, I must not seek to conceal its shortcomings in dealing with the dreadful scourge which deprives the glorious peninsula of half its charms.

Many incorrect rumours having been circulated with regard to the ransom paid for Mr. Aynsley and myself, I may here state, once for all, that the sum actually received, and divided by the brigands, was 30,000 ducats (or 5100*l.*), one-half of which has been contributed by each of us.

And while on this subject, let me express my gratitude to all those—many of them comparatively strangers to me—who volunteered pecuniary assistance in getting me liberated, assistance of which it was my good fortune not to stand in need.*

I take this opportunity also of returning my most hearty thanks to all those who, during my long captivity, so kindly interested themselves in various ways in my misfortunes, and especially to those who assisted my wife with their comfort

* Among other kind offers, the following deserves to be specially mentioned. Rajah Byjenath, having heard from my brother at Bareilly, in Rohilcund, that a large sum of money was required for my ransom, immediately offered him a draft for a lakh of rupees (10,000*l.*) to effect my liberation.

PREFACE.

and advice. Where all have been so kind, it may appear invidious to specify names, but I cannot refrain from mentioning Edward Walter Bonham, Esq., C.B., her Majesty's Consul-General at Naples, whose exertions in my behalf were indefatigable;—Signor Elia Visconti, of Giffone, near Salerno, who ran the risk of compromising himself and his family with the Italian Government, in order to assist my friends in transmitting the ransom to the brigands;—my friend, Stephen William Silver, who,—on receiving a telegram from my fellow-captive, Mr. Aynsley, announcing that 8500*l*. was required,—without hesitation, and on his own sole responsibility, placed a credit for that amount in the hands of Messrs. Cumming, Wood, and Co., of Naples, at a time when a few days' delay might have cost me my life;—Richard M. Holme, Esq., of the house of Cumming, Wood, and Co., who, in addition to other invaluable and unwearied exertions of his firm on my behalf, went to and fro between Salerno and

Giffone at very great personal risk, making the necessary arrangements for the transmission of the money to the brigands, and frequently carrying the gold about his person;—Signor Michele di Majo, of Salerno, who generally accompanied Mr. Holme on these excursions, and who frequently went alone to Giffone for us, rendering us also, in other respects, the most invaluable assistance;—and my friend H. Cowie, who came out specially from England, and bore a most important part in concerting the measures which ultimately led to my release.

I am also bound to acknowledge the kindness of the officials at Florence, and at the Foreign Office in London, who sent telegrams at all hours to my friends whenever there was news to communicate, and who were always ready to do whatever lay in their power to assist me; and also the great kindness of the Prefect, and the General in command of Salerno, who invariably showed every disposition to exert themselves to the utmost in my behalf, the latter being ably seconded by the gallant officers and men under his command.

When I calmly reflect upon the truly noble and unselfish acts that have been done in my behalf by so many persons, I feel inclined to rejoice in my past sufferings and misfortunes. Looking back on them through the bright atmosphere of the sympathy and generosity which they have called forth from my friends and acquaintances, I may well afford to treat my pecuniary loss as nothing in the scale; and thanking God for his mercy in restoring me to my friends with a whole body after all the trials and hardships to which I was exposed, I can say from my heart, now that they are past—

"Hæc olim meminisse juvabit."

CROYDON, *Dec.*, 1865.

CONTENTS

OF

THE FIRST VOLUME.

CHAPTER I.

JANUARY TO APRIL.

Palermo—Travelling Companions—Lovers of Art—The Catacombs—Monte Pelegrino—News of the Eruption of Etna—Domestic Manners of the Sicilians—The Priests—The Bombardment in 1860—The Vendetta—The Monasteries—The Grand Cemetery—Expedition to Monte Pelegrino and its Caverns—Sicilian Brigands—The Way the Palermitans manage these things—Storm at Sea—The Fishermen—Victor Emmanuel's Government—A Scientific Monk—The Value of Sympathy—The Tunny Fishery—The Campo Santo—Manner of Burial—Great Mortality among Children — More about Sicilian Brigandage . . . . pp. 3—42

CHAPTER II.

APRIL 3 TO 11.

Messina—Italian Hotels—How to avoid Disputes—Shaving at Messina—The Environs of the Place—The Camera taken for an Infernal Machine—The Prison—Taormina—Views of Etna in Eruption—The active Craters at Night—Our Servant—A Wedding at Taormina—A truly volcanic Soil—Linguagrossa—The Albergo di Etna—First Ascent of the Mountain—Our Guides—The moving Lava—Destruction of the Forests—Inquisitiveness of our Guides—The Brigands' Signs . . . pp. 45—60

CHAPTER III.

APRIL 12 TO MAY.

Linguagrossa—Second Ascent of Mount Etna—The Brigand-signs are made to our Guide—The Snow-line—The active Craters—Photography under Difficulties—My first Adventure with Brigands—A Narrow Escape—We change our Plans—A little Disappointment for the Brigands—Catania—Good Friday—Processions in Southern Italy—Change at Naples since 1860—Benedictine Monastery—Syracuse—The old Theatre—The Cathedral—The Catacombs—Fruit and Flowers—Girgenti—The Cattiva Genté—Kindness of the Consul—Our Hotel—The Excavations in the Neighbourhood—Dispute with our Host—Unexpected Decision of the Referee—Italian Officers and their Families *en voyage*

pp. 69—100

CHAPTER IV.

DIARY OF MRS. MOENS.

Ride from Salerno to Pæstum—Our Escort—The Temples—Forebodings—"Many a true Word spoken in Jest"—Our Escort deserts us—The Reason why—The Brigands at last!—The Capture—Conduct of the Italian Troops—The truly Unprotected—The Village Doctor—A new Cure for Fright—Two trying Days for Wives—Release of one of the Captives—Mr. Moens retained as a Hostage . pp. 103—120

CHAPTER V.

DIARY OF THE HOSTAGE: MAY 15 TO 20.

The Capture—The First Night's Sleep *al fresco*—Delicate Attentions — The Englishmen's Fellow-prisoners—The Captain commences Business—Value of Englishmen in Italy—Choice of Hostage by Lot—Release of Mr. Aynsley—Skirmish with the Troops—I am Detached from the Band—A Wet Night in the Mountains—Brigand Diet—Two more Fellow-captives—The Brigands' Dress and Arms—

The Ladies—Sheep-killing—Gambling—The Brigands' Anxiety about my Health—My Friends Pavone and Scope . . . . . . pp. 123—174

CHAPTER VI.

THE CAPTIVE'S DIARY CONTINUED: MAY 20 TO 27.

Brigands Merry-making — The Captain watches over me while I Sleep—His protecting Care—Thoughts of Home—A Storm—The Ladies of the Band—Doniella—Carmina—Marie—Antonina—Concetta—Their Furniture—They think I am a Milord—The Government will pay for me—A Night March—A terrific Climb — Method of selecting Sentries — Threats of Mutilation . . . . . . pp. 177—209

CHAPTER VII.

THE CAPTIVE'S DIARY CONTINUED: MAY 28.

The Second Sunday—Good News for Visconti—More Letter-writing—An Attempt at Sketching—The Englishman's Appetite—Alarms—The Soldiers—A Tradimento—Death of Luigi—Thoughts of Escaping—The drying process—Difficulty of Washing—A Wounded Brigandess—Assistance given by the Peasants to the Brigands—Description of the Band—A regular Feed, for once in a way—Pot-luck—Unpleasant sleeping Quarters—Sheep-stealers
pp. 213—247

CONTENTS. xvii

CHAPTER VIII.

THE CAPTIVE'S DIARY CONTINUED: JUNE 1 TO 7.

Wood-carving—The Wounded Girl—A Tantalizing View—Victims—The Captives not introduced—A Thunderbolt—Rain, Rain—Three under a Cloak—Ill-treatment from Cerino's Band—Their abject fear of Death—A Blow from Cerino—Consolation—New Arrivals—Screwing up—A Scrimmage with Generoso—The greedy Cerino—An Instalment of my Ransom Arrives—The Proposal to the Brigands to leave the Country in an English Ship—The Lesson of the "Aunis"—What became of the 10,000 Francs—Gambling—Viscouti is appointed my Agent—Pleasant Position of his Family—I am the only Captive—Quarrels—The Argumentum Baculinum—I am invited to Gamble . . . . . . pp. 251—285

CHAPTER IX.

EXTRACT FROM MRS. MOENS'S LETTERS: MAY 17 TO JUNE 16.

Return to Naples—Hôtel de Genève—The Coppersmiths—Telegrams to England—Letter to the Brigands—Milords or Photographers—First Letter from the Hostage—A noble Reply to a Telegram—The Second Letter—Imprisonment of the Brigand's Relatives—Arrival of H.M.S. *Magicienne*—Omniscience of the Italian Government—Sunday in Naples—Our Message stopped—The Brigandess's News—Another Letter from the Hostage—A second Instalment prepared—Letter to the *Times*—A Visit from a supposed Manutengulo—I hear of a Friend coming from England—His Arrival . . . pp. 289—318

LIST OF ILLUSTRATIONS.

VOLUME I.

PORTRAIT OF THE AUTHOR	*Frontispiece*
CAPITANO MANZO	*Title*
THE CAPTURE AT BATTIPAGLIA	page 108
THE FIGHT WITH THE SOLDIERS ON MONTE CORVINO	„ 136

VOLUME II.

THE BASILICA, AND TEMPLE OF NEPTUNE, PÆSTUM	*Frontispiece*
GIARDULLO DI PESTO	*Title*
BIVOUAC AT NIGHT NEAR CAMPAGNA	page 201
MAP, SHOWING AUTHOR'S WANDERINGS WITH THE BRIGANDS	„ 328

CHAPTER I.

JANUARY TO APRIL.

Palermo — Travelling Companions — Lovers of Art — The Catacombs — Monte Pelegrino — News of the Eruption of Etna — Domestic Manners of the Sicilians — The Priests — The Bombardment in 1860 — The Vendetta — The Monasteries — The Grand Cemetery — Expedition to Monte Pelegrino and its Caverns — Sicilian Brigands — The Way the Palermitans manage these things — Storm at Sea — The Fishermen — Victor Emmanuel's Government — A Scientific Monk — The Value of Sympathy — The Tunny Fishery — The Campo Santo — Manner of Burial — Great Mortality among Children — More about Sicilian Brigandage.

CHAPTER I.

Palermo, January 15.—On the 12th of January, 1865, we reached Palermo, after a quick passage of only forty-eight hours from Marseilles. The change from the fog and snow we left at Paris to this warm June weather is delightful. I feel my winter clothing quite oppressive, and my husband has discarded his great-coat.

Our voyage was a very pleasant one; the passengers on board the steamer were mostly Americans, very amusing and sociable; and the sea was so calm and smooth that we spent the greater part of the time on deck. The food and accommodation on board were excellent, though our last breakfast of black-pudding, pigs' pettitoes, thrushes and blackbirds, was not very tempting.

I had long conversations with some American ladies from Philadelphia, who made my blood boil by the way in which they spoke of England and the English; they considered that a very few months would now decide the war—the Southern rebellion would then be crushed, and slavery be at an end. The North was fighting in a holy cause; they had put off the war too long, and Heaven had justly punished them by making it so terrible a one, etc., etc.

On our way we steamed past Caprera, a barren-looking rock, with Garibaldi's English yacht lying at anchor near his abode.

The Bay of Palermo is more lovely to my taste than the far-famed Bay of Naples. I stood at the head of the vessel as we approached the red and stupendous precipices of Monte Pelegrino, the city, with its campanile towers and churches, surrounded by its amphitheatre of mountains, coming slowly in sight as we rounded the corner of the bay. Mount Etna, though one hundred miles off, was plainly visible, its summit entirely covered with a glittering robe of snow.

I felt unpleasantly excited as the boats came round the vessel to carry our luggage to the Dogana, for we began to have serious doubts about our chance of obtaining rooms at the Hotel Trinacria (the best in the place), especially when we heard that the Americans had telegraphed from Marseilles for apartments.

One of these (an old man shunned by his fellow-countrymen) landed with us. Both he and his old Scotch servant were characters—the master was very wealthy, having just amassed a large fortune at the oil springs, but he was as dirty and shabby as his servant, and that is saying a good deal, and neither could speak a word of any language but their own. Their first intention on starting for their travels had been to go to Jerusalem, but, falling in with the American party on board, they had accompanied them to Palermo. The Scotchman seemed terribly

upset by the change of plans, his imagination
had been so excited by the idea of visiting the
Holy Land. I pitied the poor old man, who
looked wretchedly thin and ill; his master seemed
to begrudge every penny he spent on him, and
ordered him about as if he had been a boy of
fifteen. He was generally to be seen sitting, a
woe-begone image of patience, on the luggage,
which consisted of three old carpet-bags. He certainly had no greater appreciation of the fine arts
than his master, who was once overheard telling
Robert to go into the Capitol at Rome, to see if
there were anything there that would repay him
for the trouble of visiting it. He went, but returned in a few minutes, saying, "There's
naething but a wheen naked men and women,
sir, and I'm sure you've seen eneuch o' *them*
lately; ye canna want to see ony mair." Robert's
opinion was sufficient for his master, who did not
even enter to look at the most celebrated statues
in the world.

January 28.—My husband's great amusement is in finding out and wandering over old churches. To-day I have been sitting with him among some very fine cloisters—dating from the 12th century—which have lately been discovered. We had to ascend to them through houses, as they had been entirely built up and concealed by a high wall; this wall having given way, the beautiful pillars were unveiled to view, and the cloisters are now all clear and open. We spent some hours there, enjoying the delicious balmy air, which is much softer and warmer than at Nice, or even at Mentone. I had a long conversation with the wife of the *custode* while W—— was climbing over the old walls. With the help of two men, who held a ladder supported on crumbling stones, he took some very good pictures. Yesterday I went down into the catacombs of the Capuchin convent; it was a sickening, horrible sight; we passed through long narrow rooms, dimly lighted by windows high up in the walls. The walls are covered with shelves, on which are placed glass-cases containing the dried and shrunken forms of men, women, and children, richly arrayed in ball-dresses, with wreaths of flowers around their fallen temples, and white shoes and gloves on their shrivelled hands and feet. The bodies of men, suspended by the waist, hang round the vaults; ghastly rows of priests, in full canonicals, with their servants by their sides. The inferior station in life of the latter was denoted, even after death, by the rope round their necks. I clung to my husband's arm as we walked slowly through the ghastly place, startling the cats, which rushed from under the shelves in every direction as we approached.

What a sermon this scene silently preached to us! Can we believe that, in a few short years, we may present as revolting an appearance as these horrible grinning figures? The picture is too terrible to dwell upon. It is, indeed, in mercy and in wisdom that Scripture says, "Bury thy dead out of thy sight," consoling us, at the same time, with the assurance that "The spirit shall return to God who gave it."

W—— is never weary of his photography; all our fellow-travellers envy him this amusement. I sometimes pity them as I see them lounging idly about, while time passes only too quickly with us.

January 29.—To-day being Sunday, we were present at the English service held in a large room at the consul's. The congregation numbered about one hundred. After church we walked in the botanical gardens, which are very lovely with their palm trees and other tropical vegetation. We sat and looked at the blue mountains towering in the distance.

A day or two ago we had a delightful expedition up Mount Pelegrino, to see a large natural cavern in the limestone rock: at the end of the cavern in the darkest corner stands an altar, under which, enclosed within a gilded grating, is the marble figure of St. Rosalie, represented as a lovely girl of fifteen, in a dress of solid gold, ornamented with precious stones. It was a striking scene—the dark damp grotto, the water slowly trickling from the roof, and the overhanging ferns, forming a contrast to the marble statue with its glittering ornaments, protected from spoliation by the veneration of the people. Once a year there is a grand procession of all Palermo to this shrine, St. Rosalie being the patron saint of the city.

January 30.—We have just heard that an eruption of Mount Etna has broken out. A crater has opened at the north of the *Val del Bove*, in the district called Concazze, and the lava is steadily creeping down the declivity, destroying trees and vineyards. Etna is almost entirely covered with snow.

February 12.—The Hotel Trinacria is most comfortable, and the landlord, Ragusa, very attentive. He is most particular about the people whom he admits to his table d'hôte. One Sicilian was turned away because, to my great disgust, he expectorated incessantly while sitting opposite to me at table. This filthy habit is common to all ranks in the island, from the nobleman to the lazzaroni. An English friend of ours had basins placed all round her room, with this inscription, "*Qui si sputa.*" The Sicilians and English associate very little together. The latter complain that the former are such a narrow-minded set; they think there is no place in the world like Sicily, and no people to be compared to the Sicilians. The English colony at Palermo is composed of bankers, merchants, and exporters of Marsala wine. They are very amiable and hospitable, and some of them immensely wealthy.

The English clergyman called on us yesterday

and told us a great deal about the priests; some of them, whom he knew very intimately, were highly educated men, who had travelled a great deal, but were still most contracted in their ideas. He told me it was difficult to argue with them, as their education from childhood ran entirely in one groove, certainly not the Baconian one. They start from the old axioms of the Fathers —every idea that runs counter to theirs must be wrong. A boy destined for the priesthood is placed in a seminary while still almost an infant, and taught to view everything through the one-sided medium of a strictly theological education. I wish the Church of England would open a school here. It would be permitted by the Italian government. Why should we be behind the Scotch and the French, who are working away hard in the cause of education?

We visited the museum the other day, and saw some beautiful metopes, carved stones from the tops of temples built five hundred years before the birth of our Saviour. There was a lovely statue, too, of Hercules as a young boy. We then went over the observatory, where there is, among others, a magnificent telescope just arrived from Berlin. Two astronomers were hard at work. It must be a labour of love to watch the brilliant stars in the deep blue Sicilian sky !

February is considered the best spring month here; the thermometer in our room is at 60°; and we called yesterday on a lady who picked for me in her garden a lovely bouquet of roses, carnations, and heliotropes.

The Marina, the fashionable promenade of Palermo, about half a mile long, is crowded every afternoon with gay equipages. The Italians outvie one another in the gaudiness and bad taste of their carriages. I often think it a pity that the Lord Mayor's and the Sheriffs' state carriages, or that of the Speaker of the House of Commons, cannot appear here. They certainly would be looked upon with envy, and create a very great sensation. My English friends tell me that many of the owners of these gay carriages have not a decent room to receive a friend in, and that some of the splendidly-dressed ladies would be sadly embarrassed were a visitor to call upon them in the morning, as neither they nor their houses are then fit to be seen. No one dare venture beyond the gates of the city, for fear of the brigands, so their drive is a very limited one —about two miles and a half up and down the town and the Marina. It gives me a fit of *ennui* to look at the paraders, who seem to sacrifice everything for the sake of a little display in public.

I scarcely wonder at an earnest-minded man, or woman either, retiring in disgust from the hollow worldliness of such society, and seeking a refuge in some religious house; though, perhaps too often, alas! destined to find more hollowness there than they leave behind in the world which wearies them.

ITALIAN BRIGANDS. 15

One thing often astonishes me — why the inhabitants suffer themselves to be prisoners in their town. Why do they not spend some of their superfluous time and money in clearing the environs from the brigands who infest them?*

We spent an evening with the English consul; he was most kind and hospitable, and we thoroughly enjoyed his English tea and his English fire-place. He told us some interesting stories of the siege of Palermo, by Garibaldi, in 1860. He was the only Englishman who remained in the town during the bombardment.

He one day received letters from two abbesses, begging him to come and see the mischief that had been done to their convents by the shells and shot during the storming of the town, that he might report it to the Queen of England, and ask her for redress. The consul was delighted

* When I wrote this, I little thought how deeply interested I was fated to become in the subject of brigands.

at the invitation, as it gave him an opportunity of seeing the interior of the convents.

The religious houses occupy the best situations in the town, and it will be the greatest possible benefit to Palermo when they are all suppressed, as they infallibly will be some day. There are 10,000 monks and nuns in Palermo! There is a great want of good houses in the place, and I am not the least surprised at cholera breaking out among the over-crowded, ill-ventilated habitations. I was horrified to see the places where the children grow up; the streets are high and narrow, and there are neither back windows nor doors to the houses, ventilation being entirely disregarded. Among the deaths in the obituary, half are those of children; and poor people will generally tell you that they have lost five or six children by fever. The shopkeepers pass their time lounging at their shop-doors, scarcely caring to serve a customer, and not taking the trouble to bring him different articles for selection. You must point to the shelves for what you want, and then they hesitate about taking down the article.

February 26.—The weather for the last month has been wet and stormy — for one week it rained incessantly; yesterday was clear and bright, and we walked five miles off towards Bagaria, to a cliff to gather fossil shells. We quite enjoyed being able to leave the hotel. Our Italian lessons, which we have been taking three times a week, are a great resource to us; but we find it very difficult to understand the Sicilian dialect, which is a mixture of Arabic, French, Spanish, and Italian. All the Italian o's are turned into u's, and the first or last half of the word is clipped according to the fancy of the speaker.

Our Italian master described to us a scene he had witnessed yesterday, which strongly illustrates the Italian character. He was in a church, where lay on a bier the body of a murdered man; the widow was kneeling by its side, with her little child of three years old in her arms. After a burst of frantic weeping she joined the child's hands together and made him repeat after her a solemn oath to the effect that when he grew up he would take deadly vengeance on the murderer's nearest relative. She ended by a solemn and fearful curse on the child should he fail to keep the vow he had taken over the dead body of his father. It is this spirit of revenge which makes it difficult to bring a malefactor to justice; no one will assist in convicting him for fear of the punishment that so doing might entail on the informer or his nearest relatives.*

March 13.—We are beginning to prepare for our *giro;* two or three parties have already started, who will prepare the way for us. The party

* For instances of the length to which the *vendetta* is carried in Sicily, Murray's Corsica may be consulted.

at the table d'hôte diminishes daily. We have had travellers from all parts of the world; last week some Brazilians arrived, who assured us that there is no scenery to be compared to that of Rio de Janeiro. Yesterday a Canadian sat by me at dinner, and told me that he was mortified at finding that the English knew so little of his country. One English lady had actually asked him if the Mississippi did not run through Canada! He will go back and declare that Englishwomen are so ignorant—a contrary opinion to that entertained by Italians, who have, generally speaking, a high respect for our countrywomen, on account of their superior education.

March 16.—How interesting to observe the wonderful diversity of opinions on religious matters! One lady told me not long ago that Rome was a sink of iniquity—a collection of whited sepulchres; and yesterday another, who has joined the church of Rome, gave me as a reason for her conversion that she had seen Rome, and that was enough, for it was impossible to resist the influence of a place so calm, so holy, so full of prayer!

Yesterday we sailed across the bay to see the stratum of fossil shells in the face of the cliffs exposed to the wearing of the sea; we collected numbers of them of different kinds. We then walked to an old monastery, but the monks would not admit me, though I said to them in " what I am pleased to think " my best manner, " Non posso far male." They were very polite, however, and brought me a present of citrons and limes. Many rich Sicilians are buried in large pits here, into which the body is lowered by the monks— quick lime is thrown over it, and in two or three days it is consumed. I read the inscriptions of many monumental tablets, but not one contained a text from Scripture. How thick a darkness broods over the Roman religion, as professed by the lower orders in southern Italy and Sicily, owing to the Bible—the true source of light—being so carefully kept from them by the priests! The grand burying-place of noble Sicilian ladies is within the walls of a nunnery in the town. The corpse is conveyed thither and given into the hands of the nuns, who dress it in the habit of their order, and then place it in their church, where it can be seen for some hours through the windows. It is then buried in the ground attached to the convent, to which no one is ever admitted. A Sicilian friend of ours told us that he had lost his mother two months ago. He and his brother, though poor, determined to show her every respect, and collected a sufficient sum to bury her in this place. We had a very interesting conversation with this gentleman on religious matters; he spoke very bitterly of the priests. We sent him our prayer-book to read—he returned it with many expressions of admiration at the simple and "soothing" beauty of our services.

March 18.—We have settled to make the *giro* of the island in about ten days. We hear a great deal of brigands, and are told that all the peasants carry guns, and the country round Palermo is in a most unsettled state; but Ragusa and the English consul assure us that we can go with perfect safety, as four ladies, unaccompanied by a gentleman, have just performed the tour. Before taking the grand tour, we intend making a small one round Monte Pelegrino.

March 20.—Yesterday was beautifully fine. We stepped on to our balcony, saw that Monte Pelegrino stood out clearly against the blue sky, and made up our minds to start on our expedition at half-past ten o'clock. I descended to the door of the hotel, minus crinoline, expecting to mount a donkey there, but I found it was not considered *comme il faut* to ride through the town, so we had half an hour's row to the other side of the bay, where the animals were waiting for us. To reach Monte Pelegrino, which presents to the sea a bare precipitous face about 2000 feet high, we had to cross first a carriage-road, and then some fields, thickly planted with beautiful trees. The lowest slopes of the mountain are covered with spurge—there a full low shrub of a lovely green—and cacti with stems as thick as those of our fruit trees. The road ends close by the English cemetery. There is then only a rough bridle-path, and the mountain seems advancing into the sea. All is rugged and wild—no trees, no shrubs, nothing but masses of bare rock. As might be expected, I was nervous about brigands, and my heart bounded when I saw some men with guns advancing to us. However, they were only inoffensive sportsmen, and I could concentrate all my attention again on my donkey, which stumbled at every step. We soon rounded the point, and a lovely bay was spread out before us, with high mountains in the distance, and a soft smooth turf beneath us. We by-and-bye came to a large flock of sheep and goats, and the fierce dogs guarding them rushed out upon us.

The view here was exquisite, but I could not stay to enjoy it, for we saw perched high up on the side of the precipice the cave which was the principal object of our expedition. We dismounted, and began climbing the side of the mountain. It was hard work, as the ground was covered with large, loose stones, overgrown by creepers. W—— wanted first to examine a lower cave, but as we approached it, a huge dog sprang out at the entrance, and growled fiercely at us. I steadily refused to face the enemy, and, after a little dispute, of course had my own way, and recommenced climbing vigorously, holding on tight to the end of W——'s umbrella. We heard some one calling loudly to us, but could not understand what was said. A tall, handsome man, clothed in sheepskin, with the wool outside, soon joined us, and offered to lead us to the cave by an easier path. We soon reached it, and were well repaid for our exertions. The arch of the cave was an enormous span of I know not how many feet, and about 800 feet high. Through a small opening at the top we could see the clear blue sky, with two large eagles floating in it. Great stalactites were hanging from the roof, and the sides of the cave were tapestried with beautiful creepers, and light green spurge. The blue sea was spread before us, and it was long before I could think of anything but the beauty of the scene on which I was feasting my eyes.

I was startled by the sudden apparition of another man with a gun. Our guide, divining my thoughts, introduced him as "only my companion." We sat down to eat the few biscuits we had brought with us. This seemed to excite the compassion of our guides, for they immediately offered to lead us to *their* cave, which they did with tender care, breaking down all the creepers in my path, and making the way as smooth for me as possible. They placed rough seats for us, covered with their cloaks, and spreading a pocket-handkerchief as a tablecloth, laid out upon it a loaf of bread and a kind of scalded cream, called *racotta*. They entreated us to eat, and we sat by the fire enjoying the scene, surrounded by the four dogs and two men, who talked very readily to us. They remarked with wonder my complexion and W——'s as being so very different from their own. They told us they were shepherds, and this cave was their home. At last, with great regret, we left them, thanking them for their hospitality, and leaving the money, which they refused to take from us, on their pails. We then returned to our donkeys, and riding through La Favorita (the King's gardens) reached our hotel about five o'clock. We brought away with us a few fossil teeth and small bones with which these caves abound. W—— employed two men a few days ago to dig up an enormous shoulder-blade for him, but it broke and cut his finger badly. The cut has since festered, which has damped his ardour in collecting fossil bones.

March.—My fears were not unfounded. The day after our expedition, on the very road we had traversed with such pleasure and security, a Sicilian gentleman, driving with a friend, was carried off by brigands. He was quite close to the town, when a break with two horses drove swiftly past him, turned sharply round, and drew up right across the road, stopping his carriage. Eight men with guns jumped from the break, surrounded the carriage, and carried off the Marchese Guccia, telling the friend, whom they mistook for a servant, to return to Palermo' and procure a certain sum for his master's ransom. The papers took scarcely any notice of this affair. They merely mentioned that Signor Guccia was sequestered by *malfattori*. He was liberated in a few days, either by payment of the ransom or through the interest of some rich proprietor said to have power over the band. I made many inquiries, but the whole affair was soon hushed up, and I could obtain but little information.

The indifference displayed rather shocked our English notions. I could not help thinking of the storm of indignation that would be excited in England were any gentleman in North Devon or Wales, or even in Ireland, to be unceremoniously separated from his family, and forced to pay half or perhaps all his fortune to be restored to them. These atrocious affairs seem to be matters of every-day occurrence here. Only a few weeks ago another case occurred (not mentioned by the newspapers), in which I was so much interested, that I used to go almost daily to the consul's, to hear if the poor man had regained his liberty. A Signor Salemi, returning from Monte Maggiore, near Bagaria, had gone two or three miles, attended by two *bordenari* in front, and his own armed servant behind, all on horseback. They

were stopped by twenty armed horsemen. The
two *bordenari* were allowed to escape, but Salemi
and his man were blindfolded and taken half-an-
hour's march into the country. The man was
then sent back with a message that 1500 ounces, or
750*l.*, were required by the band. Madame Salemi
the next day collected half the amount, which was
returned to her with a message that it was not
sufficient. In a fortnight the required sum was
procured. It was received, counted over, and a
receipt sent back by the brigands. The next
morning at daybreak, Signor Salemi was placed
in the middle of a field, blindfolded, and com-
manded not to remove the bandage until a signal
was given. When he took it off he did not know
where he was; but seeing a cottage at a distance,
he went to it and roused the inmates. They gave
him food and a bed; and in the afternoon he
was taken to Monte Maggiore. He was so weak
that he could hardly stand, as they had given
him nothing to eat but bread, herbs and water.

He had lived entirely in the open air, and was kept blindfolded the whole time.*

We have had several thunder-storms; and sometimes I get nervous about earthquakes, for Monte Cuccio, the highest mountain here, is an extinct volcano. At times, rumblings and groans are heard, making one feel that it may break out at any moment. Yesterday there was a change in the appearance of the sky; a mist hung over the sea, grey as the heavens, but all was still and calm when the fishing-boats went out as usual in the afternoon. We were walking down the

* During the six months from January to June, several other gentlemen have been taken in the neighbourhood of Palermo, and among them Signor Bergami, a most respected corn-broker, and a good friend to all the peasants, who was taken four miles from Palermo. When the brigands surrounded him Bergami drew his revolver, which missed fire, but at the same instant one of the thieves thrust at him with a dagger, wounding him in two places. That was the extent of the mischief done in his case, for the police turned up at that moment, causing the thieves to run away. Scarcely a week passed without a fresh instance, but not one-fourth of the cases are ever heard of. It is only when a man of note is taken that any fuss is made.—W. I. C. M.

ITALIAN BRIGANDS. 31

street, when there came on such a gale that we were forced to rush home immediately. We saw from our windows a most exciting scene: the sea was covered with enormous waves; all the little vessels were trying to come into the harbour, it seemed impossible for them to live in such a storm. The poor fishers' wives and children assembled on the beach, watching with fearful anxiety, each tiny little bark. I was thankful when they one by one got into port, and the poor women went home rejoicing over the safety of their husbands and sons. A French Admiral Fitzroy had written to warn the fishermen of this coming Levanter, as these sudden storms are called; but they, too like many of our own maritime and fishing population, are so self-willed that they gave no heed to the warning, and the storm found them unprepared.

It was the king's birthday a day or two ago; flags were hung out, but there was a very poor illumination. It is no great wonder if his Government be not popular amongst the poor, as so many new taxes have been levied, and the young men are taken away for two years to serve in the army, though the last arrangement is greatly to their advantage, for they are kindly treated, taught to read and write, and to hold themselves erect. They see, too, a little of the world beyond the boundaries of their own town and village, and return to their homes, at all events, with less contracted notions than when they left them.

March 30. — The storm has changed the weather; it is lovely to-day, and very hot. The thermometer is at 70° in my room. My husband has been out all day at Monreale, a beautiful old monastery, built in the year 1182 by William of Sicily, and Joanna, sister to our Richard Cœur-de-lion. He has been taking photographs of the cloisters. I did not go with him, as no women are allowed to pass the gates of the monastery. The monks, of the Benedictine order, all belong to noble families. They lead anything but a secluded life, as they keep carriages in which they drive about Palermo, and they take in all the newspapers, &c. They invited W—— to dinner. The wine, grown in their own vineyards, was, like the other constituents of the dinner, excellent. One monk, a very handsome, intellectual man, became a great friend of my husband's. One day I went up to Monreale, where I was introduced to him. We had a long conversation together, in the course of which he told me he never regretted becoming a monk. I asked him if he ever suffered from *ennui*. "No, never! I am constantly occupied, when not engaged in the offices of religion. I employ my time in constructing a steam-engine, a machine to fly through the air, &c.; but this is a great secret, for not one of my brother monks knows of it." Happy man! to be so contented. I often think, with Goethe, that the happiest man is the cobbler, who sings at his work.

A titled English lady is working hard here, doing all the good she can, and trying to persuade the Sicilian ladies to visit their poor sisters, who have to struggle with poverty, sickness, and, too often also, with unkind and cruel husbands, and ungrateful children. Oh, if women only knew how often, by a gentle word of sympathy, a disheartened, broken spirit might be soothed, an embittered, over-burdened heart softened, nay, even a soul rescued from despair, and strengthened to struggle again with renewed vigour in the hard battle of life! Hundreds in this world hunger and thirst after this little help, which could be afforded them with ease if women would but feel—

> "A sense of an earnest will
> To help the lowly living,
> And a terrible heart-thrill,
> If you have no power of giving;
> An arm of aid to the weak,
> A friendly hand to the friendless,
> Kind words, so short to speak,
> But whose echo is endless—"

noble words, in which rings an echo of the feeling that inspired the Preacher when he told the whole world that " Heaviness in the heart of man maketh it stoop, but a good word maketh it glad."

March 31.—Palermo is like an oriental town. The shops are open and without windows, and you may see the tailors, shoemakers, tinmen, &c., plying their several crafts almost in the open air. For nearly a month they have been selling strawberries, green peas, &c., in the streets. The climate far surpasses my expectations; it is exquisite, and so is the scenery. The only drawback is the difficulty of getting into the country, but this does not seem to trouble the inhabitants. No one, not even the cobbler's wife, walks. The great amusement of all is to be driven slowly up and down the town, which can be done for fivepence. They are all astonished at our English love of exercise. We started the other day to walk round Monte Pelegrino, but got caught in a heavy shower of rain at the little fishing village of Virgine Maria. The peasants asked us into a cottage, about twelve feet wide, and very long, half filled with the tunny nets they were making and preparing for the arrival of the tunny fish in April.

The large nets are made of grass spun into the thickest string, which they net without needle or mesh, simply twisting it round their fingers. The nets, when set, extend for nearly a mile—sometimes further. The tunny fish, which is a perfect monster of the deep, something like the porpoise in shape, and from four to eight feet long, is driven from chamber to chamber in the nets till it enters the *corpo*, or chamber of death. When the captives are all collected there, the work of death commences; all the boats of the fishermen for miles round, with much formality at first, but soon in indescribable confusion, surround the fish and slaughter them by hundreds with their spears, till fish, boats, and men are all half smothered with blood. We were told that it was one of the most horrid spectacles that could be witnessed.

On our way home we passed the Campo Santo,

or common burial-place of the town. There is a sufficient number of vaults to allow of one being opened every other day. The dead, to the number of twenty or thirty (in a town of 200,000 inhabitants), are collected every day, and at twenty-two o'clock, or two hours before sunset, they are thrown in; quick-lime is scattered over them, and the vault sealed up till its turn comes round again in a year. We met several bodies being carried on the way to their long home. The coffins are not shaped like ours, but are simply oblong boxes, sometimes black, but generally red and green, with coloured effigies of saints painted on them.

Half the deaths are among very young children. You may constantly see a man walking along very quickly with a small red oblong box, slung behind his shoulders by a piece of cord; he reaches the dead-house, puts the box down outside the door, opens the lid, and takes the body carelessly out. If it has clothing on worth anything, the attendant harpies seize it as their spoil, and then throw the corpse on the ground while the box is carried back by the man who brought it. We saw one body being carried in a black sedan-chair by two men, who, before going up a little hill, left the body in the middle of the road while they went into a wine-shop to drink. After the dead are taken from their homes, the relatives never see them; there is no service read over them; the priest simply sprinkles the bodies with holy water before they are flung down a hole two feet square into the vault beneath, in a few hours after which lime resolves them into their primary elements.

The English burial-ground joins the Campo Santo, but is very different. It is filled with flowers, ornamental trees and shrubs, with a large stone opposite the gateway, on which are inscribed texts from the Holy Scriptures in English and Italian. The monuments, with their words of holy comfort and hope, give a very different impression to that of the Italian ones, where one never reads anything but a long catalogue of the virtues, real or imaginary, of those to whose memory they are erected.

March 29.—We intend starting for our *giro* tomorrow. Many of our friends have advised us not to go, others tell us that it is quite safe, as English people are never taken; but when I ask them "would you go?" they seem to think that is quite another affair. As I mentioned before, neither the rich Sicilians nor the English residents dare drive half a mile out of the town. I do not know why the tourists and people belonging to the hotels are safe. I sometimes think the hotel-keepers pay black mail to the brigands— the people stopping with us at the Trinacria took long expeditions over the mountains, and were never molested. W—— and I take long walks into the country and always return safe— a thing no Sicilian would do. The gardener of the Palazzo Serra di Falco told us that his mistress rarely came now to see the garden, in which she had formerly taken such delight; though it is not more than a quarter of an hour's drive from the town!

We were told the other day the story of the

capture of Mr. ——, an English merchant, two or three years ago. He was driving with his daughter about a mile from Palermo, when the carriage was suddenly surrounded by six men, who threatened to shoot him if he did not get out of the carriage quietly and go with them. He pretended at first not to understand them, and spoke to them in English; but they said "it is no use trying to deceive us; you can speak Sicilian quite as well as we can, Mr. ——; come with us directly." He, seeing resistance was useless, went with them, leaving his daughter in the carriage with the coachman, surrounded by men who kept pointing their guns at them if they dared to move. The bandits dragged poor Mr. ——, who is a large, stout man, over walls, fields and ditches, until at last he fell through fatigue, and said he would go no further. They then all sat down, and began steadily bargaining with him for his ransom. He was to sign a paper for 1000*l*., but this he positively refused to do. They then asked 500*l*., which he

declared he would not give; then 200*l.*, and at
last it was settled that he should bring 50*l.*
himself on the following morning, and deposit it
on a certain stone in a field which they pointed
out to him. He was then allowed to depart, after
solemnly promising that the money should be
forthcoming. Poor Miss —— sat in the meantime in the carriage in the most terrible anxiety,
crying bitterly—the brigands hid themselves behind the wall, on the top of which the muzzles
of their guns could be seen pointing at the carriage. She did not dare drive on, as the brigands had told her if she did so it would be at the
peril of her life. A priest and some other men
passed, but took no notice of her; at last a cart
drove up with several men armed with guns sitting in it. They stopped and asked Miss ——
why she was in such distress; she told her sad
story, and they advised her to drive home directly,
as it was dangerous for her to stay outside the
town. She tried to persuade them to follow the
brigands, and to rescue her father; but this they

steadily refused to do. They kept entreating her to drive on, but she said she dared not do so, as the guns of the brigands were still pointing at her. She wanted to point out the guns to these men, but they immediately hushed her with gestures of great alarm, and drove away. She at last, summoning up courage to follow their advice, drove swiftly back to the town, to carry the sad news to her family ; the soldiers immediately turned out and scoured the country. Mr. —— returned in the evening. Many men were taken up on suspicion, and thrown into prison. Mr. —— was asked to go and try to identify them ; this was endangering his own life, however ; for had he been the instrument of their conviction, their relations would have shot him—so he declared he knew none of them, and they were consequently released. In a few days several men called on Mr. —— to thank him, and his watch was returned to him.

CHAPTER II.

APRIL 3 TO 11.

Messina—Italian Hotels—How to avoid Disputes—Shaving at Messina—The Environs of the Place—The Camera taken for an Infernal Machine—The Prison—Taormina—View of Etna in Eruption—The active Craters at Night—Our Servant—A Wedding at Taormina—A truly volcanic Soil—Linguagrossa—The Albergo di Etna—First Ascent of the Mountain—Our Guides—The moving Lava—Destruction of the forests—Inquisitiveness of our Guides—The Brigand Signs.

CHAPTER II.

Messina, April 3.—We got very tired of Palermo, and as the weather was so bad that it was useless to attempt the giro along the roads, we took the steamer at five o'clock one afternoon, and arrived here at six o'clock the following morning. It has been raining hard to-day. We seem persecuted by bad weather, as in March it rained for twenty-four consecutive days. Our hotel (the Trinacria again) is comfortable, and the charges very moderate—twenty francs a day, including servants and candles, a sitting-room and bed-room. We settled the prices with the landlord before we agreed to remain. The only way to get on at the Italian hotels is to bargain beforehand. Those who pay the price demanded are despised as well as imposed upon.

This town is quite a modern one, as it has been frequently destroyed both by earthquakes and bombardments. It is now a thriving seaport, full of life and activity; nearly all the steamers trading in the Mediterranean put into the harbour, which is sheltered by a strip of land in the shape of a crescent. The view across the straits, with the mountains of Calabria in the distance, is charming, and I am never tired of watching from my window the animated groups collected round the fine fountain on the opposite side of the road. Above the fountain is a colossal statue of Neptune, calm and majestic, looking as if he had just risen from his watery realm. His large beard is dripping, and at his feet, chained, lie two large female figures, representing Scylla and Charybdis, with faces distorted by passion.

The barbers here ply their busy trade, and seem hardly to have time to attend to their numerous customers, every coachman, tailor, and beggar of the town coming here in turn to be shaved. The dirtiest old beggar, with only a few straggling grey hairs on his head, his body covered with filthy rags, will sit down in the sun, and, with upturned face, give himself up to ten minutes of thorough enjoyment, while a gentle and dexterous hand lathers his withered cheeks, and with a sharp razor removes all " superfluous" hairs, and sends him back again to society, if not a better at least a cleaner man.

April 4.—We have just returned from a delightful expedition to a very old abbey, built in the middle of a torrent, about three miles from the town. The water has washed such a quantity of rubbish into it that its beautiful doors and pillars are nearly buried. On each side of the torrent rise high walls of rock, overshadowing the building. We sat here for two hours, and I amused myself by watching the women climb the steep sides of one of these mountains, with large baskets on their heads, their heavily-laden mules following them. To my dismay, I was told that, when the pictures were taken, I should have to climb quite as steep a hill. While W—— was photographing, several young men passed, and I asked them to stand to enliven the pictures, but they all declined, and evidently thought that the camera, on which they looked with the greatest fear, contained an evil spirit. They had never seen such an apparatus before. At last I persuaded one bolder than the rest, and W—— took his portrait standing against the picturesque old building. When the pictures were all satisfactorily taken, the basket containing the apparatus was put on the back of a donkey, and we began to ascend the hill. It was a regular clamber, but I was well repaid by the magnificent view when we reached the summit.

The Straits of Messina, the snow-capped mountains of Calabria, and the town, with its strong fortresses, were all mapped out before us. On the other side was the blue Mediterranean, stretching far away to the horizon. Stromboli and the other Lipari Islands were plainly visible, the former puffing up tall columns of smoke. I sat down to rest on the short sweet turf, and could scarcely tear myself away from the lovely scene. Our carriage met us here, and we drove back to Messina by a zig-zag road down the mountain, catching, at intervals, the same beautiful view, while, on one side of the road, were large groups of trees, banks of moss and wild flowers in profusion, cyclamens, enormous violets, and quantities of white heather. The air was perfumed by the sweet scent of the flowers.

April 5.—Yesterday we visited a very old tower called Rocca Guelfonia, and had to go through part of the prison to reach it, four or five soldiers escorting us; it was a sad sight to see the prisoners staring at us like wild beasts from behind their iron gratings, which are often double. Some were walking up and down for exercise on a very small roof with iron railings all around. Many of the faces made one shudder, every evil passion seeming to have set its seal upon them. The soldiers had all honest, open countenances and gentle manners, and would not accept the money we offered them, neither would they allow the porter at the gate to take any. I saw such young children, not more than five or six years old, working hard at breaking stones, or leading horses, and engaged in many other kinds of work.

Taormina, April 7.—We engaged a very good carriage with three horses for twenty francs a-day, which was to include all expenses, and drove along the coast to this place. The road, which winds close to the sea, is very lovely, bordered by orchards, some in full leaf, others in blossom, their pink flowers standing out in bright relief against the snowy background of the mountains. The country is thickly populated, and we drove through numbers of villages, the houses generally of stone, two stories high, but without glass in the windows, which were closed with wooden shutters only. The people looked very happy and industrious, with honest, good-natured faces; the young girls had all fine features, but very dark complexions. We went into one house where they were making vases and jars; my dress as I went in upset two large ones at the doorway. I expected to hear the smash, but, on looking round, saw that the jars had merely altered their shape, and were all bent on one side, the clay being still wet and pliable. Our hotel has only just been opened in the centre of the town; the accommodation is miserable, but the view magnificent, with Mount Etna exactly opposite the window; but alas! the pleasure to one sense is counterbalanced by the misery to another, for one of the black streams so common in Sicily, into which runs all the drainage of the town, flows down the middle of the street, just under our windows.

We can get no meat here, nor anything eatable except macaroni. The town is eight hundred feet above the level of the sea; the road up to it is a very steep ascent, and was only made a year ago by the command of Prince Humbert. The view from it is very fine, and we were fortunate in having a clear day, which allowed us to see Mount Etna towering in its lofty grandeur to the height of eleven thousand feet, its summit and great part of its base covered with snow, and volumes of smoke ascending from the crater. We saw two new cones which looked at night like huge bonfires. This view of the mountain is most sublime; it seems to fill nearly the whole horizon, standing alone in all its unearthly might. We could scarcely sleep the first night, but stood at the window watching the flaming cones.

We spent yesterday at the old Greek theatre, which is built on a high hill; the pillars are of granite, which must have been brought from Egypt, as there is none in Italy. We have engaged a servant who speaks tolerable English; he is most handy and useful, and generally looks neat, although he contrives to travel without any luggage, carrying not even a small bag.

The dirt is terrible, but so it is everywhere in Sicily. We carry our own sheets with us, made in the shape of bags to tie round the throat. Without this precaution we should never have slept at all, nor would there have been much of us left by this time.

April 9.—The town was in a state of great excitement to-day, on account of the marriage of the richest man in the place with a young girl who came straight from the convent to the church. After the ceremony, she changed her dress, and putting on a gay red jacket, a hat with feathers, &c., paraded, with the bridegroom, up and down the town, her friends walking in procession behind her. We met them, and bowed to the bride, who was not at all pretty.

We have just returned from a lovely walk. The sun had sunk behind the hills, but still lighted up the top of Mount Etna, gilding the transparent smoke which rose from the crater, and floated away in fantastic wreaths above the clouds which hung in dark masses below. We were walking in a deep valley, between the mountains, covered with trees and vineyards. A stream ran far beneath us to the sea, which was of the loveliest and deepest blue, the white sails of the boats looking like large sea-birds floating over the surface. The blackbird, now heard for the first time since I left England, was singing sweetly: all else was hushed and calm. I cannot describe the soothing influence of the lovely hour and scene. On reaching the water the charm was broken by the horrible smell rising from it, or rather from the mud and water-plants which grew by it, whose fetid odour often occasions destructive fevers.

This side of the island is most fertile and densely populated. After the lapse of years has rendered the lava brittle and easily pulverized, vegetation will spring up luxuriantly, and villages are built over the ashes of former ones, the inhabitants thinking little of the ruin that may, at any moment, overwhelm themselves.

On every side of the mountain are cornfields and vineyards, and luxuriant groves of olive and almond trees, planted on land entirely reclaimed from the lava, which crops out now and then in all its hideous blackness and sterility, either in low mounds or huge rocks, whose bare and rugged sides mark the course which the river of molten fire took centuries ago, destroying ancient corn-fields and vineyards, as fertile and beautiful as those which now rejoice the eye with their luxuriant growth. "Everywhere by the side of present happiness and wealth we see the phantom of past desolation and misery, making us tremble for the future." Trouble and sorrow are so like this lava; they sweep over the human heart, leaving it to all appearance bare and scorched like the sides of the mountains. Years roll by, and as from the lava-covered plains rich fruits spring up in all their luxuriant beauty, so, "though now chastening seemeth not to be joyous but grievous, nevertheless afterwards it yieldeth the peaceable fruits of righteousness."

April 11.[*]—Having determined to make a close inspection of this new eruption, which had broken out during the month of January, and had continued incessantly ever since we started from Taormina at six o'clock in the morning, in

[*] The narrative is here taken up by me from my diary.—
W. I. C. M.

a carriage with three horses harnessed abreast, according to the custom of the country. We had been strongly advised not to stop at Piedimonte (where most of the people who had visited the new craters had taken up their quarters), but to go on four miles further, to an equally miserable town rejoicing in the name of Linguagrossa, supposed to be derived from the rustic dialect of its inhabitants.

The course the lava was now taking rendered it necessary for all those starting from the former town to go round to the westward of the district devastated by the fiery stream; and to do this, the four miles of road to Linguagrossa had to be traversed, which we thought might be done more comfortably in a carriage than on the backs of mules. At Linguagrossa we took up our quarters at the Albergo di Etna, and we soon came to the conclusion that Linguagrossa was the most miserable looking collection of houses we had ever seen. Not only were the houses black from being built of lava, but everything was black, land and all; the soil was nothing more than the lava pulverized by the action of the weather on it for centuries. One hill, however, to the north of the town, was an exception, being composed of red lava, which only served to make the rest of the land around look blacker.

Our arrival seemed to afford great amusement to the crowd lounging about the door of the hostelry. They were especially diverted with the weight of my wife's portmanteau, which required two men to carry it, as it was half filled with glass ready for pictures, my dutiful wife having, in a most exemplary manner, sacrificed half the space allotted to her wardrobe for the sake of her husband's negatives.

We had been rather dismayed at the hotel at Taormina, but on entering the Albergo di Etna I confess my heart sank, and A—— looked the picture of despair. We had the choice of two rooms, each of which had beds in all four corners; and

we were told that if more travellers came, we
should have to share our room with the new
comers, but this we declared impossible; so the
spectacled landlord said as there was a lady in
the case he would break his rule for once. The
best room, looking into the street, was declared
uninhabitable on account of the fearful smell of
burning fat occasioned by cooking on a *braciera*
or pan of live charcoal, which is the only fire
used among the natives of Sicily. A table was
carried into the other, and we waited impatiently
for our dinner, which was being cooked, while the
landlord was ordering and preparing the mules
and guides to go to the *nuovo fuoco*, as the place
of the eruption is termed.

We arrived at 12·30, and by two o'clock we
had despatched part of the tiny saddle of mutton
we had bought *en route*. (It never does to trust
to the resources of a town in this part of the
world on the first day of an arrival.) On the
announcement that the mules were ready, we

descended into the street, and found four animals and three guides—the head guide, we afterwards learned, was a brigand, under whose care our party was considerately placed by the landlord, who told him he would be held responsible for our safety. He was a most villanous-looking fellow—of most abhorred aspect, "by the hand of nature marked, quoted, and signed to do a deed of shame." He was accompanied by a boy, and a very good-looking youth about twenty years of age, who devoted himself to A. all the time.

The first three-quarters of an hour we passed between lava walls, the land on either side cultivated in a rough style as corn-fields, filbert-woods, or vineyards. We noticed too, that although the vines at Taormina were beginning to show the new shoots, here, at 1800 feet above the level of the sea, they did not give the slightest signs of the approach of summer. We passed along deep ravines—or lava-nullahs (if I may be allowed to use such a word) chiselled out by the fiery torrents in days gone by, the appearance of the country growing blacker still, and wilder, as we ascended. The winter torrents had, in places, cut the solid lava into curious ridges parallel to each other; while scattered about were many craters that had caused devastation hundreds of years ago.

Sixteen hundred feet above Linguagrossa the woody region begins, the forests consisting of enormous oak trees. Here were congregated a number of charcoal-burners, who lived in rude huts, on which were placed branches of fir trees to keep off the rain, and outside each hut was a large block of snow placed on a slab of lava; the water from the snow, as it thawed, dripped into a barrel. The men were exceedingly wild-looking, and had very large axes which they were wielding vigorously, but all ceased their labours to watch our cavalcade pass by. I observed that they had fierce dogs for their companions, like the men on Monte Pelegrino.

The *scorza*, or track, was here so steep that A—— had at times to cling to the neck of her mule. We now saw firs mingled with oaks. The latter, according to my aneroid barometer, did not grow at a higher altitude than 2600 feet above Linguagrossa (or 4325 feet above the level of the sea). Some of these oaks were very large, being fifteen feet in circumference. The firs were also of great size, being nine feet round, and rising straight up to a great height.

After continuing our adventurous way through this lonely region for the space of two hours and a half, we heard the noise of more woodcutters hard at work. These proved to be men engaged in saving the trees that were in the line of the lava's course. The stream was now moving fast down the mountain, having advanced one hundred yards since yesterday. My barometer at Linguagrossa reported 28·50, my thermometer 58°; here the former showed 25·60, the latter 42°, indicating that the spot where the molten stream had arrived was about 4725 feet above the sea level.

The first sight of the moving mass of lava was truly marvellous, and baffles description. In some places it was a mile wide, and about twenty-five feet high, and from the main stream ran a number of smaller ones, like huge railway embankments. The surface of the side towards us was black in colour, and as the mass swept on in its remorseless march with horrible crackling sound, lighting up the grand old trees before devouring them, the upper surface was gently raised by the molten matter running underneath, and the *scoria* fell over the sides, emitting a fearfully lurid glare.

It was difficult to approach very close, on account of the intense heat. I detached a piece of red-hot lava with a long stick, and forced a franc into it to keep as a memento of our visit, but in one minute it swelled up, and, passing off in fumes, disappeared, while all the natives laughed at our looks of dismay.

We saw several large firs that had been enveloped by the fiery stream, and as we watched we saw them fall with a crush, their trunks having been eaten through by the hot lava, and they were then carried with the stream on the top of the scoria. I noticed that when the lava lost its red heat, it was still impossible to break it, from its tenacious character; but as it grew cold it was quite brittle. The scoria here was not in very large pieces like that of Mount Vesuvius, where it is in shape of slabs, but was in roundish lumps from six inches to a foot long. Just above where we were the lava had taken a sharp turn, and it was expected to run down a valley full of large trees; the owners of the wood were here with fifty men, cutting down and dragging the stems out of the expected course of the devouring element. Oxen were attached to the logs in a curious way; a bar was simply placed under their humps, and to the ropes from this were fastened large spikes, which were driven into the wood. The faces of the proprietors showed their distress of mind, and they complained bitterly of the ill-fortune that had overtaken them; luckily, however, they had buyers for the wood they were cutting, as the new railway from Messina to Catania required large quantities of it for sleepers.

It was with great difficulty that we tore ourselves away from this scene of new sensations; but we were getting faint with the great heat, and it was late, and we did not wish to run the risk of being out in the dark in this wild region. Before leaving, however, we quite made up our minds to visit the mouths of the new craters the next day, which were two hours' climb higher up the mountain, the lava having already run about ten miles from the mouth of the fissure, where it issues from the mountain side. It was twenty minutes past five, when we turned our faces homeward; we soon experienced the discomfort of riding down places almost as steep as a staircase, but the mules were surefooted, and we could only hold on tight and trust in Providence.

On our way down the head guide explained to me the brigands' signs, which are always made

to each other in meeting. The eyes twisted to
the left and a slight toss of the head upwards,
show that the travellers are of the same trade,
and that some work is in hand; the hand extended, with the fingers turned up, meant "take
him prisoner;" the same, with the fingers turned
down, signified "kill him." Our guides were
very curious to know whether the *signorina* was
going up to the *bocce* to-morrow,—which route we
should take, and where we were going afterwards.
I was annoyed when I heard that our man,
Giuseppe, had told them to Randazzo. We had
contented ourselves with saying Catania, to which
town there were two roads, without informing
them that we intended to choose the one through
Randazzo.

It was dark an hour before reaching our
resting-place, but a moon, nearly at the full,
helped us on our way, and, arranging for fresh
mules the next day, we went early to bed in
order to prepare for the hard work before us.

CHAPTER III.

APRIL 12 TO MAY.

Linguagrossa—Second Ascent of Etna—The Brigand-signs are made to our Guide—The Snow-line—The active Craters—Photography under Difficulties—My first Adventure with Brigands—A narrow Escape—We change our Plans—A little Disappointment for the Brigands—Catania—Good Friday—Processions in Southern Italy—Change at Naples since 1860—Benedictine Monastery—Syracuse—The old Theatre—The Cathedral—The Catacombs—Fruit and Flowers—Girgenti—The Cattiva Genté—Kindness of the Consul—Our Hotel—The Excavations in the Neighbourhood—Dispute with our Host—Unexpected Decision of the Referee—Italian Officers and their Families *en voyage*.

CHAPTER III.

April 12, 1865.—The next morning we were up by five o'clock, having spent rather a sleepless night from the excitement of seeing what we had talked about so long and with so much interest. We made as good a breakfast as we could manage to procure, and at about six started again over the same ground as yesterday. There was to-day another mule on which was placed the square basket, containing my photographic apparatus, which was at last secured, after great wrangling among the four men who accompanied us. Two of the guides were the same as yesterday, and the others were brothers of the good-looking youth (by name Pepi), who attended so carefully to my wife's safety.

When we had been on our way about half an

hour—passing numbers of women carrying heavy loads of wood—we met two men carrying axes in their hands. I saw them make the signs to Pepi, which I had been taught the day before, including the extended hand, whereupon I laughingly said "all three alike." They looked rather surprised, and replied, "you know too much." I did not like this at all, but as the two men were going towards the town, I determined to go on, keeping, however, a sharp look-out all the way up. About two miles from the spot where we had seen the lava yesterday afternoon, we turned off a little to the right, passing through the dense forest of fir trees; and here we first noticed the ground covered with a fine black dust, which had been carried by the wind from the new craters. We now came to the snow line, and great care was necessary in passing the ravines, all of which were full of soft snow, in which the mules sank to their knees, and it required great exertion on the part of the guides to extricate them and get them over safely. The dust got thicker and thicker as we ascended; we passed a large tract where all the branches of the trees had been consumed by fire, leaving the gaunt stems blackened by its action.

At about ten o'clock we reached Monte Crisimo, an old crater, about 150 feet high and very steep. On ascending this, the scene of devastation and fury of the elements burst on us; it was a fearful sight, and the awful roar proceeding from the then active craters completely deafened us. The smoke rose in dense masses, but fortunately a northerly wind blew both it and the stones and dust, which were constantly being thrown up, away from us in the opposite direction.

About one hundred yards from the crater on which we were was the lava that had already destroyed all in its course. Here the mass was from forty to sixty feet high, and according to our guide extended one mile across. It was a curious sight, its whole surface cracked and distorted into all kinds of shapes, bearing upon it numerous trunks of trees that had succumbed to the force of the fiery stream, and now lay extended like giants on its cooled surface.

The longer we looked the more awe-struck we became; the two nearer craters were belching forth steam and smoke, making a noise like that of great waves breaking on a shingle shore, or like the noise of all the engines in the world letting off their steam, while a lambent sulphurous vapour kept playing over various circular patches on the northern sides. This vapour appeared by daylight a yellowish colour, but at night we were told it was a dull red flame.

The smoke was not constant, but rose every five or ten minutes. It would come up in dense clouds and curl round the craters, and then in two or three minutes rise in the air leaving the two mouths visible, which were in the form of perfect circles with one side depressed. I took two views from this spot, using the water which the men had brought up with them, (as they thought for drinking purposes). As I was finishing the second picture, I saw, to my dismay, the two men we had met before with axes approaching, but now they were armed with guns. I immediately sent Giuseppe, our servant, to A——, who on seeing the new-comers retreated to the top of the old crater. The two men now came up and began whispering to the guides. I at this put my hand in my side-pocket, so as to be ready to use my revolver at a moment's notice if requisite: and, not to appear afraid, I approached the new-comers and said a word to them, when to my delight they said " good-day," and left us.

I now took another picture, and A—— came down from the hill to me. In a few minutes who should appear but the men who had just gone away ! but this time they had five or six more with them, all armed as the others, and wearing belts round their waists. These men all came and stood close behind me as I had my head under the black cloth, while developing the view of the lava I had just taken; and I do not think a photograph was ever taken under more disturbing influences! I really did not know what to do; and, to get them away from the position they had taken close to me, I made Giuseppe, who was in an awful fright and pretended to be asleep, tell them to sit down a little way off, while I, without their knowledge, took a capital picture of them.

A——, fortunately, had not the slightest idea what these men were, and as a joke she sat down by them, pretending to be a captive in the hands of brigands. Little did she think that, instead of a joke, it was reality, and that these men had come up all this way on purpose to rob and murder us, thinking I was an engineer, because of my photographic apparatus and barometer. In this part of the world, all engineers are considered millionaires, for the ignorant people think that they are the persons who employ so many hundreds of workmen, and that they make the railways with their own private funds. Fortunately, as we afterwards found out, our guides had felt the weight of our luggage at the inn in the town below, and Giuseppe having told them that we were going to Randazzo, they thought it would be more profitable to take us, luggage and all, the next day, while on our road in the carriage. We now had luncheon, and when this was eaten, I had the satisfaction of seeing our new friends depart, but only after a great deal of confidential talk with the men who had come up with us.

I now insisted that we should be taken nearer to the mouths of the craters, to which at first the men would not agree; but, on my persisting, we started off on foot, two of the guides carrying the photographic-box. We walked along the side of the lava for nearly a mile over the snow which here lay on the ground, though covered with the black dust from the eruption, to the depth of from four to twelve inches. The first layer of dust had been live ashes, some of them an inch each way in size. It was very closely packed, and would probably keep the snow from thawing all the summer. Pepi and I supported A—— between us, all three of us sometimes sinking in the snow to our knees. At last we found out that it was only where the dust was wet that the surface was unsafe, and after this discovery we got on better.

As we got closer, the wild grandeur and thunder of the mouths increased, and the noise was fearful, quite stopping all conversation. A little to the west of the two most active craters was a hill or rather mountain, 1000 feet high, that had been thrown up (as we were told) in two or three days, at the commencement of the eruption. This was quite black in colour, with patches of yellow (probably sulphur) in several places. From the summit of this large crater light vapour was always ascending, and, every now and then, enormous black clouds of smoke would cover the top. The wood, in this direction, had suffered much, only the tall stems of the fir trees being left, where the lava had not utterly destroyed them. It was a most wild and desolate sight, and made fine studies for my camera, by the aid of which I secured, with great difficulty, some very striking views.

The work was most fatiguing, for I had to go to expose the plates at least 300 yards from where I had put up the developing-box, and running over the treacherous surface of snow and dust was most tiring. I do not think that any amateur ever worked harder. I felt, however, that I should never have such a chance again, and was stimulated by the knowledge that no one but M. Andrieu, whom we had met at Messina, had ever photographed such a scene, and by the wish of sustaining the honour of England, by getting, if possible, better negatives than those which my rival had shown me. On completing my labours, I was so exhausted that I drank with avidity a little distilled water, which I found among my chemicals, and I would gladly have given a Napoleon an ounce for some more. It was now time to return, but before doing so, we took one more look at this wild and fascinating scene. Behind the great crater to the left, Mount Etna raised its lofty head, about 5000 feet higher than the spot where we were, covered with the purest snow, listening in majestic silence to the roaring of its youngest born.

The new eruption had taken place just at the termination of the woody region. Five craters in all, we were told, had given vent to the subterraneous fires, but, at the time of our visit, two of them had ceased to be active.

We now hurried back to our mules, and packing all our *impedimenta*, mounted, and began our course homeward.

The excitement of the craters had in the

interval made me forget the brigands, who, I felt sure, were not far off; but the behaviour of our guides now renewed my apprehensions. Instead of talking to me continually as before, they were quite silent, and would hardly answer my most trivial question, and they were constantly wandering on each side ahead of the party. I do not think I ever spent a more uncomfortable time; for uncertainty is worse than reality; and my anxiety was not made more pleasing by one of the men saying to me, "*Mi piace molto la signorina!*" It was a great comfort to me that A—— had not the slightest idea of my fears, which I did not tell her till our arrival at Catania next day. At 7.30 we reached our little inn, and, after having supper, we were soon fast asleep.

April 13.—When we first arrived at Linguagrossa we had arranged with our coachman for a visit to Randazzo and the other towns at the back of the mountain. We were talking about this ex-

pedition after our return from Mount Etna,
when our man, Giuseppe, entered the room, and
closing the door mysteriously behind him, as if
afraid of being overheard, entreated us, in a
whisper, to give up our projected visit to Randazzo, as he had heard that the men whom he
had seen the day before were brigands, and that
they had arranged a plan to take us and our
luggage on the road. The poor man turned
white with fear as he spoke. We told him,
laughing, that he need not be alarmed, as the
brigands only captured Italians, and never English travellers. He then ran over a long list of
the people who had been taken, and told us that
even the inhabitants of Linguagrossa knew we
were very rich persons, for "all could see that
the Englishman was an engineer, or the next
thing to it, viz., a nobleman! for was not the
white turban he wore round his hat a sign of his
riches or rank?" The landlord added his advice
to Giuseppe's entreaties, telling us plainly that

he could not guarantee our safety unless we took an escort of soldiers. Being determined not to let anyone know the road we were to take, I dismissed them with these words, "Tell the coachman to be ready to start at eight o'clock to-morrow morning." They both left the room, shrugging their shoulders at the madness of the Englishman. I, however, from the moment I had been surrounded by the men near the crater, had resolved to return to Catania by the coast, and to give up the expedition round the mountain.

The next morning, early, Giuseppe came again to implore me to drive to Catania, but all that he could get from me was the order to tell the coachman to get the carriage ready for the luggage. Poor Giuseppe obeyed with many a doleful sigh and shrug. The carriage drove round; the horses' heads were turned towards Randazzo; the bells had been taken off, that no warning of our approach might be given; the coachman looked pale and nervous, watching the crowd that assembled to see us off; I stood on the balcony while the luggage was being packed; and when all was ready, we descended and stepped into the carriage; and then, standing up, I said to the coachman, "Turn the horses' heads, and drive to Catania." A loud roar of laughter broke from the crowd as we drove furiously away, feeling sure that no intimation of our change of purpose could have been conveyed to the brigands in time for them to interfere with us. They probably spent this day in lying in wait for us in some dark wood, or convenient angle of the rocky road between Linguagrossa and Randazzo.

April 13.*—We arrived at Catania on the 13th. The drive from Linguagrossa was beautiful, but the distant view of Catania, which is on a flat plain at the foot of Mount Etna, did not prepare us for the beauty of its splendid build-

* From Mrs. M.'s diary.

ings. It forms in this point a striking contrast to many of the Sicilian towns we have seen, which are generally lovely at a distance, from their picturesque situations, but dirty and miserable when once the gates are passed. Catania is a comparatively modern city, having been built about two hundred years ago, after the overthrow of the old town by one of the many earthquakes which are always threatening the towns and villages around the giant mountain whose smoking crater is to be seen towering above from every street. The houses, which are really enormous, are entirely built of lava and stuccoed over, and the wide streets are paved with it. Catania is a flourishing, thriving place, and the trade will be immensely increased when the railroad is finished round the coast, connecting all the principal towns. Englishmen will probably then find that this is a charming winter residence, as it is very healthy, and the country round is lovely.

There are very interesting remains of the old Greek and Roman city disinterred from the lava, especially the remains of the theatre and the catacombs; but we were not able to visit the latter, neither could we make any of the usual expeditions round the mountain, for which Catania is the starting-point, on account of the ill-health of my husband, who was almost entirely confined to the hotel during our stay in the place.

On Good Friday, at six o'clock in the evening, there was a grand procession of the senators, monks, noblemen, and principal people in the town. They first assembled in the Cathedral, which was brilliantly lighted up, and assisted at a solemn requiem. The general public were not admitted, so we took our stand on the Grand Piazza outside, and after waiting a short time, the great doors of the Cathedral were flung open, and the procession slowly defiled from it, headed by the bishop and canons in quaint copes and hoods lined with ermine, with long fur trains. A crown of thorns was the only head-dress worn, and every one carried an enormous wax-taper, the monks chanting a solemn dirge the while. In the centre of the procession was a wax figure of our Saviour lying on a bier, the blood slowly trickling from his side. For two hours they slowly marched about, whilst a solemn silence reigned around; awe and devotion were imprinted on the features of the crowd, almost as if they were present at the awful event itself instead of its scenic representation. The most striking incongruity in this solemnity was the conduct of the street boys, who ran in and out of the procession, picking up and carefully treasuring the pieces of wax that dropped from the lighted candles.

The popularity of these processions is a sort of measure by which to gauge the moral and intellectual progress of the people. Among the ignorant population of the remote towns of Sicily, they are frequent, and are considered to bring a blessing on both town and people; whereas in Southern Italy, even in Naples itself—once the abode of the most abject superstition,—these ceremonies are becoming every day rarer. The entry of Garibaldi into the latter town was the first ray of the flood of light, which is destined, I trust, to illuminate all the dark places of this lovely land. Instead of processions, he gave the people schools, which are eagerly attended by a people so long systematically kept by their rulers in the grossest ignorance. I was grieved to hear that the Church of England, both at Palermo and Naples, is doing little or nothing; while the Lutherans and Presbyterians have established Sunday-schools, depôts for the sale of bibles, &c.

But I have wandered too far away from Catania and its churches. We paid a visit the other day to one of the largest in the world—that belonging to the Benedictine monastery. It is unfinished, as, on account either of an earthquake, or of some fault in the building, the pillars have sunk, and the foundation is considered insecure. We heard high mass, and I was rather amused at seeing the care the priests took to avoid cold in their numerous prostrations. Every time they lay flat on the floor (a ceremony I had never before observed in any Roman Catholic Church), a rich carpet with a velvet pillow was spread on the ground, while the poor and scanty congregation were compelled to content themselves with the hard, cold stone floor.

After the service we walked round the church, and I stopped to admire two magnificent bouquets of the loveliest flowers on one of the altars. The priest, seeing my admiration, stepped forward, and, to my surprise, politely invited me to take any I liked. I hesitated to do so, and he collected for me a bouquet of the most splendid roses, heliotropes, white tulips, violets, &c. In the meantime W—— visited the museum. I was only allowed to enter the chapel. The monastery is extremely rich, but there are very few monks. We then visited the ruins of the old theatre. Curiously enough, they have discovered that, under the Roman theatre was an old Greek one, the excavators having laid bare the enormous blocks of stone characteristic of Grecian architecture. We saw little else in the place on account of my husband being attacked with illness; and directly he was well enough to travel, we took the steamer for Syracuse, where we arrived on the 20th.

Syracuse, April 24.—We are now in far-famed Syracuse. I am enchanted with the place. No wonder that the Greeks, with their keen love for the beautiful, built their city here, for the situation is so striking, and the harbour splendid. There is every probability that it will be the chosen station for the fleet of United Italy. This town brings the power of ancient days vividly before me.

The cathedral is built out of an old temple to Minerva. The enormous Doric columns, built six hundred years B.C., are still to be seen embedded in the walls. No modern columns can be compared to these, so gigantic and severely grand. Once or twice the earthquakes have striven to dislodge them, and have succeeded so far that some have been thrown on one side and off their base. Everywhere a column, a ruin, an old wall tells of the days when the Greeks were lords here.

We met the other day an English clergyman, the Rev. J. C. Murray Aynsley, and his wife; and yesterday, after reading the servic together, we all went for a long ramble, and when tired, rested close to the shore, under the shade of enormous fig-trees, through whose clustering branches we could see the deep blue sea. Above us a nightingale was singing most melodiously, and the ground was everywhere enamelled with flowers of the most brilliant hues. At our feet—for we sat on a little hill—were the ruins of the Temple of Diana. Columns, statues, white marble steps, all lay scattered about. We sat and gazed till my heart seemed to overflow with thankfulness at having been permitted to see such a lovely scene.

We left it with deep regret, and then continued our walk, in the course of which we descended into the catacombs, which extend their subterraneous ramifications for miles and miles. There were but few inscriptions and only one or two frescoes. They are larger and more regular than the catacombs at Rome. The walls in the galleries have large arched openings at regular intervals, leading to passages cut far into the limestone rock, and containing numbers of stone coffins of all sizes, once covered by slabs, which have all disappeared. This city of the dead awed and chilled me to the heart. After the long, damp passages, the sepulchral gloom, the thick, close air, I was glad to ascend again into the land of the living, to bask in its warm, bright sunshine, to breathe the sweet perfume of its flowers and trees.

"We rested again in a very bower of Arcadian sweets, where Flora was still in her prime." The ancient quarries are turned into gardens—and such gardens! Here, for the first time, I saw the orange and lemon trees in their natural growth, not topped and trimmed to produce fruit, but trees of a splendid size, covered with bloom and fruit. The air was deliciously scented by these and the beautiful rose-trees (really *trees*), geraniums and fig-trees. Surrounded by cliffs hung with creepers of every bright and lovely hue, we lingered long in this sweet spot, until evening, creeping softly and slowly over the landscape, warned us to return home.

Girgenti, April 27.—We left Syracuse on the 26th by the weekly boat. Mr. and Mrs. Murray Aynsley travelled with us, and after a smooth passage of twenty-four hours, we came in sight of the harbour of Girgenti, which is not deep enough to admit the steamer; so we were forced to land in a little boat —to my eyes dangerously overladen with the weight of the boatmen, our four selves, the luggage, and Giuseppe and his personal belongings (consisting of a pair of socks we had given him) tied up in a pocket-handkerchief.

As we approached the pier, three or four wild-looking men sprang into the boat and almost overset it. A regular fight now began for our luggage; fortunately the boatmen took our part in the dispute that ensued. I stood a little apart, keeping close to two of the gens-d'armes, whose loaded revolvers bore witness to the truth of what we had been told at Palermo—that whoever comes to Girgenti must expect to meet *cattiva gente*. The luggage was at last put on a truck and wheeled towards the Dogana, but here, as elsewhere, owing to the *lascia passare*, kindly given us by the Marquis d'Azeglio, it was not examined, and W.'s negatives escaped the rough handling of the custom-house officers.

We now looked round for some means of conveyance to the town, which we saw proudly towering on a hill about four miles off. Its appearance at this distance, with its castellated buildings and lordly mansions, enchanted us—a charm soon to be cruelly dispelled on a nearer view. We heard at the Dogana that there was no carriage here, and that we must send to Girgenti for one. Poor Giuseppe, greatly against his will, was despatched on this errand; I do not know whether the long walk up the hill or the fear of brigands weighed most on his mind. He started at twelve o'clock, and we sat on chairs placed in the open air for us, and whiled away the time talking to the head of the Douane, who, like all other officials we met with, seemed thoroughly discontented with his position. One o'clock came, two, three, four; we grew wearied and hungry, and the gentlemen went in search of food while we kept guard over our boxes. They returned with a little bread and cheese, and then wished to go in search of Giuseppe, but we were too much afraid of brigands to allow them to leave us. Five o'clock came, no Giuseppe; but at six, just as we were giving up all hopes of his appearance that night, we saw him coming slowly towards us with a doleful face, and the unpleasant information that there were but two carriages in the town, and both these were engaged. The hotels, too, were full, and not a room to be had in the place. We were fairly at our wits' end, when, happily for us, the consul drove by, and seeing our disconsolate position, offered to take us to the town, while our husbands walked with the small cart which had been secured to carry the luggage.

After a wearisome drive up the steep hill, we entered the old gateway, and passing through the crowd of people lounging round it, drove to the consul's through the filthy streets. After fruitless endeavours to get apartments at one of the hotels, we accepted the offer of an old man to let us two rooms. We were led down a narrow alley, and picked our way in disgust through black pools of water, emitting the most villanous odours. The rooms were dirty and miserable, but we were so worn out with fatigue that we were thankful for any shelter. Just, however, as we were discussing how we should manage, Giuseppe came to tell us that a guide, to whom W—— had shown some kindness at Palermo, offered to give up his room at the hotel to us.

Thinking we should be more comfortable there, we accepted the offer, but were not much better off, for the window looked into an alley similar to the one which led to the old man's house, and the door opened into the salle-à-manger, where eating was going on all day long, and into which, when supper was over, the servants brought planks, turning it into a well-filled sleeping room—so that our chance of obtaining fresh air was very small. We were obliged to remain, as the steamer called at Girgenti only once a week; and we were told it would be madness to attempt a land journey across the island to Palermo. We could only do it by engaging a very large escort of soldiers, and even then there would be every probability of our being attacked and perhaps taken by the brigands; so we made the best of our situation, and engaged a carriage to take us early every morning to the Temples, where we spent the whole day, enjoying the pure air and exquisite scenery. I used to lie down among the red clover, feasting my eyes on the beautiful ruins, all of which are on rising ground commanding a view of the sea on one side, and the wide plain thickly planted with almond trees, just then in their tender spring beauty, on the other, the picturesque town crowning the summit of the lofty hill, and forming a fitting background to the picture.

May 2.—We invited the consul and his family to a pic-nic yesterday, and passed a very pleasant day. The town, despite its dirt and smells, is very amusing, for the inhabitants live in the streets, where they discuss their own and neighbours' affairs with the utmost energy. To-day we went to the sulphur mines; but I having learnt, by former experience in Tyrol, to dread the atmosphere of a mine, declined accompanying the others in their descent. They came back horrified at the sight of children of from six to twelve years of age, toiling under loads of from 70 to 100 lbs. We afterwards visited the excavations carried on by Mr. Dennis. Nothing of any importance had been discovered, though tombs and ruins of houses are scattered all over the fields in the neighbourhood of the town.

Our week passed quickly, and the morning of our departure arrived. We began to think we should have a little trouble about settling our bill, as we had not been satisfied with the conduct of the landlord, and W——'s greatcoat had been stolen from the hotel. Our fears were verified; a most exorbitant bill was brought, everything being charged half as much again as we had paid at the best hotel in Palermo, and many things put down which we had never had. Mr. Aynsley and my husband determined not to be imposed upon; but to their surprise, the landlord, at the first objection made, said "Refer it to the English consul." They accordingly went, but were surprised at this gentleman's supporting the landlord in his attempt at imposition. They would not give in, and returned to the hotel, where we were waiting in the carriage. They then laid down the proper amount, due according to the tariff of prices established everywhere in the island; and, as the coachman refused to drive on, and a crowd assembled round us, we got out and walked, our luggage having been sent on in the morning. We had not got half-way down the zigzag path cut in the hill, when we saw the landlord and some of his men pursuing us. They came up with us, vociferating and gesticulating fiercely, and some one, pretending to be an official, stopped our luggage; we appealed to the vice-consul, who took our part; but, fearful of losing the boat, the gentlemen consented to pay an extra napoleon, and we embarked, feeling that the reputation of the inhabitants of Girgenti was a well-earned one.

The boat was crowded with soldiers, officers and their wives, the latter all young and very pretty, and it was most amusing to see one mamma after another, when tired of her baby, handing the little creature over to a great, tall soldier, who walked away with a grim smile of satisfaction overspreading his countenance, as the baby clutched vigorously at his moustache and gay cap. I heard afterwards that these soldiers were the only nurses the babies had, and most efficient and tender ones they proved.

I could not help thinking that this certainly was an advantage for the soldier. His being brought into such near contact with ladies and children must humanize him. The enlistment of the young men for soldiers, instead of being, as the ignorant peasants think, a great hardship, is, on the contrary, a very great benefit for them. The poor ignorant boy is taken away from his village, where he has grown up in perfect ignorance, and besides having his mind opened by contact with others, fares altogether far better than if he were to remain all his days at home.

Soon after this we left Sicily for Naples, where we arrived without experiencing any adventures worth recording.

CHAPTER IV.

DIARY OF MRS. MOENS.

Ride from Salerno to Pæstum—Our Escort—The Temples—Forebodings—"Many a true Word spoken in Jest"—Our Escort deserts us—The Reason why—The Brigands at last!—The Capture—Conduct of the Italian Troops—The truly Unprotected—The Village Doctor—A new Cure for Fright—Two trying Days for Wives—Release of one of the Captives—Mr. Moens retained as a hostage.

CHAPTER IV.

May 19.—When we had been a few days at Naples, we thought of starting again on our tour, and accordingly, on the 14th of May we travelled by rail from Naples to Salerno, intending if possible to pay a visit to the renowned ruins of Pæstum. We put up at the Hotel Vittoria, and next morning we started on our proposed excursion about 8 A.M., having received the most positive assurances both from the authorities at Naples and the hotel-keeper at Salerno that the road to Pæstum was perfectly safe* and guarded by soldiers throughout.

Our party consisted of Mr. and Mrs. Murray Aynsley, my husband and myself. As I got

---

* In the Appendix will be found a copy of the notice which was posted up in the Hotel Vittoria.

into the carriage, I said in English, "I hope we shall escape the brigands." To my surprise the porter answered me in my own language— "Oh, no fear, lady, the road is safe; parties are going every day from here to visit the temples." I had no real fear for myself, but merely made the observation in joke, as I had always done when starting for any of our expeditions in Sicily.

The road from Salerno to Pæstum is most uninteresting; no hills, nothing but a dusty plain. We had three horses to our carriage, with the usual accompaniment of jingling bells. How I hated the sound of bells afterwards! They always brought back to my mind this dreadful day. We were escorted the whole way to Pæstum by soldiers, who joined us on the road, when a little distance from Salerno, asking our coachman where we were going. Although they thus accompanied us, they did not warn us of any danger, notwithstanding that (as we afterwards discovered) they were fully aware of the presence of a band of brigands in the neighbourhood, two Italian gentlemen having been captured by them a week previously. We arrived at the temples at eleven o'clock, and spent the whole day among them, my husband amusing himself in taking photographs of them, one of the carabineers being all the time in the temples in attendance on us.

The day was hot and sultry. I could not walk a step without feeling ill from the intense heat. We occupied ourselves in trying to find relics of the past, in a place where some workmen were excavating. Mr. Aynsley picked up a ring and some marble fragments. Two Germans here joined us, and we formed a plan for returning together, but fortunately for them, this plan was frustrated by the wilful delay of our coachman. After we had taken tea, it being then half-past four o'clock, and the carriage having been ordered at three, the gentlemen grew tired of waiting, and went in search of the coachman whilst I reclined on one of the large piles of stones, and admired the extreme beauty of the scene before me, with which at first I had not been so much impressed. I looked through the massive columns of the ruined temples at the wooded plain beyond, with the mountains towering in the distance; but a dark cloud seemed over all. A feeling of melancholy crept over me, a foreshadowing, I suppose, of some coming sorrow.

The carriage at last arrived, and we were all glad to get into it and drive away. The road was quite deserted, our escort of the morning having disappeared—in fact we did not see a single soldier, and the authorities allowed us to return without any warning or guard, although they knew the danger we were running in so doing. We heard afterwards that the troops were drawn off on purpose to allow negotiations to be carried on with the band of a brigand named Giardullo, for the ransom of Signors Bellelli and Magnone.

We soon began talking about the brigands again, and Mrs. Aynsley and my husband kept trying to frighten me by pointing out dangerous places. However, I never for a moment felt that there was real cause for alarm, and so we talked and laughed about the brigands just as careless unthinking people talk about their own death, never realizing the possibility of its being at hand. Mrs. Aynsley and W. were in high spirits, and at last, tired of teasing me, told me that we had passed all the dangerous places, and one wood in particular that had been always notorious as an ambush.

I was very tired, and so fell asleep, but was suddenly roused by hearing Mrs. Aynsley exclaim, "Here really are the brigands at last!" I started up and saw, as it seemed to me, the fields on both sides of the road covered with armed men, some like serpents creeping through the standing corn, and advancing swiftly to the carriage; others rising in all quarters—from out of the corn, and from behind the tall hedges. They all closed noiselessly round the carriage, pointing their guns at us. One man seized the horses' heads, and turned them across the road. The coachman did not attempt to drive on. No one spoke. We were completely surrounded. There could not have been less than thirty men! I whispered to my husband, "Give me your watch. I can hide it." This watch, which he much prized, he slipped behind the cushions of the carriage, without answering me. Still not a word was spoken. I said something, I know not what, to the man holding the horses' heads. He did not reply, but the brigands all made signs to my husband and Mr. Aynsley to get down. Silently the coachman descended, and let down the steps, saying "*scende.*" Silently my husband and Mr. Aynsley got out: the armed men surrounded them, and quickly marched off with them, one of the brigands whispering to the coachman to stay there for a quarter of an hour.

The Capture at Battireglia

Till then I had been bewildered, looking on what was taking place as a dream.

I now first realized what was happening, and a strong determination came over me that I would not be separated from my husband. I sprang out of the carriage and rushed after him for about twenty paces, but the brigands instantly formed a line to prevent my following, and my husband and Mr. Aynsley turning round implored me to return. I felt powerless, and two brigands gently and courteously led me back to the carriage, begging me not to be afraid, as they would return with my husband in a quarter of an hour.*

Once back in the carriage, my head reeled, and I nearly fainted. Mortal fear came upon both Mrs. A—— and myself. All we did at first was to pray, then we looked at one another and asked what we were to do. We hoped and thought the brigands would carry our husbands behind a

* The brigands afterwards told my husband that my conduct was "madness."

house not far from us, take their money, rings, &c., make arrangements for paying a ransom, and then send them back to us. We had heard that this had been done with Mr. ——, when he was taken by brigands at Palermo some years ago. We kept gazing at the house, and constantly saw people coming towards us. Alas! they were only peasants, more than a hundred of whom passed while we were waiting in fearful expectation, but no one took the slightest notice of us.* My heart seemed to stand still.

About a quarter of an hour had passed, when suddenly we saw a cloud of dust along the road and heard the feet of horses galloping furiously. "The soldiers!" exclaimed our coachman, and, as they were passing us, we stopped them, with the terrible news, "The brigands have taken our husbands!" "Which way?" they asked. We pointed to the house, and away galloped about

* At least fifty were looking on when the brigands surrounded us.

thirty soldiers in hot pursuit. We now thought that as the brigands were on foot there must be an instant encounter, and our husbands would be restored to us.

Half an hour passed—then an hour—but no signs of the soldiers; nothing but peasants passing along the road, on their way to their homes. Hope began to leave us. It was now seven o'clock; the night was drawing on, and at last we reluctantly made up our minds to leave the spot, and to drive on to Battipaglia, the nearest village; there we stopped to consult about our going on to Salerno, as the coachman was very averse to our proceeding farther that night. I, too, thought it better to stop, if possible, where we were, as I had a large number of circular notes about me, my husband having the letter of indication. A crowd surrounded our carriage, but none showed signs of sympathy. We asked the most respectable looking man if there was any place where we could pass the night. He pointed to a wretched-looking house —one of the stations built to accommodate the soldiers and their horses.

There was a room over the stables which we were told we could have, and we were advised to pass the night there. I must confess that by this time my own nerve had given way, and I longed to hide myself from the gaze of the curious crowd. We asked every one, " Have you informed the soldiers?" " Have you alarmed the country ?" We were assured that messengers had been sent in every direction with the news.

One man, the best dressed in the crowd, kept talking vehemently to Mrs. Aynsley. I could not hear what he said; but I thought that he was perhaps the owner of a good house, and was offering us shelter for the night. Mrs. Aynsley rebuffed him, and when we had driven into the stables, I asked her " why she spoke so crossly to him ?" She told me he was the village doctor, and so importunate in his entreaties to be allowed *to bleed us*, that she was at last obliged to speak sharply to him. I looked at her colourless face, and felt that mine presented the same appearance, and thought bleeding a very unnecessary operation. The Italian doctors, however, would seem to be disciples of Doctor Sangrado, as they always have recourse to his favourite operation, after any great excitement.

A kind old peasant woman now advanced, to show us the way to our room; we mounted a ladder, and found ourselves in a loft, half filled with hay, with a large heap of Indian corn in one corner—in another a hen sitting on her nest. There was but one small window, which I opened directly, as the room felt oppressively hot and stifling. Our hostess gave us water with snow in it, which was most refreshing, and brought some clean sheets and a night dress for Mrs. Aynsley, who immediately went to bed. Three or four women came to us; amongst others, a poor creature, whose own husband had been taken, and who came, as she said, "to mingle her tears with ours." I reciprocated her kind feelings, and would gladly have talked with her, but the presence of strangers was irksome to Mrs. Aynsley, who begged me to get rid of them; so I told them the signora was ill, and they all quietly retired. I then tried to make some tea with Mrs. Aynsley's apparatus, when the door again opened and some men came in. Amongst them I saw the sullen face of the coachman, whom we afterwards strongly suspected of having been in league with the brigands. They gave us the good news that the brigands were surrounded, and could not possibly escape.

They went away, and were succeeded by two young officers, with several of their men. How our hearts sank when the first question they asked us was—"Which way did the brigands go?" We answered, "Why, we told you at the time, round by the white house." "We cannot find them," was the reply. "We have scoured the country, our horses are worn out, and we must rest two hours before we go out again." "Have you alarmed the country?" we asked. "Are the soldiers guarding the roads to the mountains? Have you sent intelligence of what has happened to Salerno and Eboli?" Over and over again they assured us that everything had been done; that telegrams had been sent; that the mountains were well guarded; all the soldiers called out; the brigands could not escape, &c.; but they failed to convince me, and my heart sank. I wept bitterly, as all hope of seeing my husband left me. The officers were kind-hearted men, and tried to comfort me. They begged us to keep up our courage as they wished us good night, promising to go out again in two hours' time in search of the band.

I could neither lie down nor sleep, but sat at the window, looking at the scene outside. The soldiers were leading their horses to the water, or sitting in groups, smoking and talking together. A wandering musician, with a concertina, went from group to group, listening to their conversation, and after a time crept quietly away. I firmly believe that this man was a spy of the brigands, as I noticed that he did not play any tune correctly—he was only trying to discover what were the plans of the soldiers for the morrow. After a time the soldiers retired to rest, and Mrs. Aynsley asked me to read to her. I had Fenelon's *Conseils* with me, and read a chapter or two to her. (This small book I sent afterwards to my husband.) She fell asleep, and I returned again to my window.

It was a lovely night; the stars were clear and bright. At about three o'clock the soldiers led out their horses, and after about an hour's preparation, they mounted and galloped out of sight. Still too wretched to sleep, I sat at my window, thinking that the morning would never dawn. I could see the roads to Pæstum and

Eboli, along which numbers of peasants passed, either on foot or in the rough country carts. At last the stars disappeared one by one, and the welcome sun rose. I extinguished our curious old lamp, and we prepared for our return to Salerno. The officers had promised us an escort, and we waited some time for it; but as no soldiers appeared, we determined to proceed alone. The broad daylight, the numbers of people passing, renewed our courage, and we again took our places in the carriage, after thanking and rewarding our kind hostess.

On our way we met two or three carriages, the occupants of which we warned of the danger attending their expedition to Pæstum. They of course gave it up, and turned back.

We determined, notwithstanding our dusty condition, to drive direct to the General's at Salerno. The coachman at first demurred; but, as we firmly insisted, he was obliged to take us. We trusted that the General would be able to give us some news of our husbands; we never for a moment suspected that we should be the first persons to convey to him the intelligence of their capture, after seventeen hours had elapsed since it took place. We were shown into a large drawing-room, and in a few minutes General Balegno appeared. He looked rather surprised at seeing two ladies, who could hardly speak for weeping. We told our story, and great was our dismay when we found that he was utterly ignorant of the fact of two Englishmen having been carried off in broad daylight on the high road from Salerno to Pæstum—a road supposed to be perfectly safe and guarded by the soldiers under his command. He instantly rang the bell, summoned two of his staff-officers, and gave orders for such and such detachments of soldiers to be sent out in pursuit, and not to return until our husbands were free, or the brigands prisoners. Having despatched these officers, he turned to us, and begged us to be comforted, as all would soon be well.

In the evening we had many visitors, coming to offer their help and sympathy. A deputy of the Italian Parliament entreated us to send a telegram to Florence to rouse the Italian Government, and to beg for help against the brigands. Another gentleman, a resident at Salerno, came to comfort us by telling us that he too had been taken by the brigands, and had escaped from them unhurt by paying a ransom. We were just retiring for the night, when a messenger arrived with a letter for Mrs. Aynsley, containing the joyful intelligence that her husband was free, and would be with her early the next morning, the brigands having liberated him to raise the ransom for my husband and himself.

I was dressing the next morning when Mrs. Aynsley rushed into my room, exclaiming, " Good news! Good news! they are *both* coming ! I have seen them in the carriage." I rushed out into the passage; the stairs and landing-place were crowded with people. I saw Mrs. Aynsley in her husband's arms. I gazed, oh! how eagerly, into all the faces that were turned towards us, but I did not see the one I looked for, and I returned into my room with that deadly feeling of disappointment which makes the heart sick. I sank on the sofa. Mr. and Mrs. Aynsley came into my room, but for some time I could not speak to them; at last I managed to shake Mr. Aynsley's hand warmly, and congratulated him on his escape; but I had not the heart to ask him how it was that he had returned alone, and that my husband was still with the brigands.

He then proceeded to tell us his adventures, which will be found fully detailed in my husband's diary.

CHAPTER V.

DIARY OF THE HOSTAGE, MAY 15 TO 20.

The Capture—The first Night's Sleep al fresco—Delicate Attentions — The Englishmen's Fellow-prisoners — The Captain commences Business—Value of Englishmen in Italy—Choice of Hostage by Lot—Release of Mr. Aynsley—Skirmish with the Troops—I am detached from the Band—A Wet Night in the Mountains—Brigand Diet—Two more Fellow-captives—The Brigand's Dress and Arms—The Ladies—Sheep-killing—Gambling—The Brigands' Anxiety about my Health—My Friends Pavone and Scope.

CHAPTER V.

May 15.—We had ordered the carriage to be at the temples at three o'clock, but it did not come till four. We had nearly reached Battipaglia, observing, to our great astonishment, that there were no soldiers about as in the morning, when all at once, about five miles from Scafa, the ferry over the River Sele, we saw a number of men creeping out of the corn on the east side of the road; they pointed their guns at us, and quickly coming up to the carriage, turned the horses across the road. More men now advanced, and the coachman got down, opened the carriage door, saying, *Scende*. Mr. Aynsley and I had to get out, I having instinctively taken off my watch and left it in the carriage.

We were dragged away at once, but on looking

back I saw to my grief that A—— had jumped out and wanted to come with me; she was stopped by the brigands, who said to her, "*Non avete paura, Signorina, non avete paura.*" I wanted to return for a minute, but the brigands would not let me. We were hurried away up a lane on the west side of the road towards the sea, past a house. (The carriage was stopped near wood carts, on the top of one of which a man was placed to give notice when we were coming. We had passed these carts near the river in the morning.) Almost immediately after leaving the high road, Luzzo, a proprietor living at Battipaglia, was taken by the brigands; and a minute after a young man, who was seen about 200 yards off in a field, was also captured.

We were then pushed along at a fast pace towards the sea, over fields, and through thickets, the best path always being left for us. When at last we were allowed to rest a little, the captain of the band (whose name I found to be Gaetano

Manzo) gave us each a very large cloak, called
a *capote*, usually worn by the peasants, to sit on.
We took this opportunity of asking the captain
what he wanted with us? He rubbed his right
thumb and finger together, and said "*Denaro ;
non temete.*" I asked how much further we had
to walk. The answer was "*Lontano, lontano
assai.*" I, joking, said I hoped he had horses to
carry us. He nodded his head, "*Si, si.*" They
were all very kind in their manner, always ad-
dressing us as "Signori," putting a strong accent
on the last syllable. We rested about ten minutes,
and Luzzo, shivering a great deal, asked for a
capote, saying there was much malaria about.
We also put on our *capotes*.

Soon after starting again we had to pass several
wet places. It was getting dark when we came to
a river (the Tusciano) running very fast, about ten
or twelve yards wide. They carried us over on
their shoulders, and we rested again on the other
side and drank some water. Here I tore up my

letter of indication, as well as a letter of introduction to one of the principal bankers at Naples, and other letters, thinking it more prudent to do so than to keep them about me. I put the pieces into my gloves and threw them away as opportunity offered.

On we went again, passing over swampy ground and deep ditches, which we jumped easily, much to the amusement of the brigands, who cannot jump. They laughed heartily at our agility, and still more heartily when one of their own party fell into a ditch. When we were near the sea we passed a house, and one man who was sent to visit it brought back a quantity of dark-coloured hard dry bread, in shape like small penny rolls. These were distributed, and we walked on again for some time, and presently came to cultivated land. It was very dark now, and we could not see our path by the side of a running brook, so they gave me a long stick, which was a great help. We passed near some houses, dogs barking as we approached. Two or three men were sent on in advance, and we were placed in the centre of the band, who all walked in Indian file.

The advanced guard were making signals continually. The brigands' peculiar call note is made by uniting the tips of thumb and forefinger of left hand, and then kissing loudly the third joint of the forefinger. We were often stopped till the road was considered secure. As it was getting towards midnight the caution increased, and when we neared the main road still greater vigilance was exercised, and we halted while the great highway was examined. We were then taken across. The same precautions were used when we approached the Eboli road, after crossing which we came upon a patch of cabbage and onions. "*Pigliate*" was the command from the captain, and the spot was soon stripped. A little hard cabbage was handed over to me, with some garlic, which I put in my pocket.

On we went past a large farm house. I looked

out for a chance to escape, but they saw as well by night as by day, and had we attempted to have left the ranks our fate would have been to have had a few shots sent into us which would have left our bodies a prey to the worms. We halted before daybreak on the banks of a rapidly flowing stream, and we were told to lie down and go to sleep among some osiers. The ground was very damp, so we objected and were allowed to sleep on the dry bank; but at daybreak we were made to descend and conceal ourselves with the band. Branches were stuck in the ground to make the cover thicker.

As I was lying fast asleep, I was awakened and startled by feeling a man's hand pass over my chest and ribs. My moving disturbed the man, and he left me. I mentioned this to Mr. Aynsley. We did not like it at all; I was so tired, however, that I soon fell sound asleep again. Mr. Aynsley was not so fortunate. He told me the next morning he could not sleep after this incident. I believe now the man was trying to find if I had a pistol. My first night's rest in the open air was excellent. I little thought how many I should have to pass far less comfortably before I saw a bed again.

The first operation in the morning was to collect all the bread and then divide it into shares. We were treated like the rest. The bread was so hard that they soaked it before eating it. They now continually asked us about our property. At about eleven o'clock we made a move, and walked in Indian file through a highly cultivated country.

After two hours there was a halt, and the captain asked us how much money we had at Salerno. We told them our stock of gold, but they would only believe in our being rich lords. They wanted also to know what was the matter with my hands. I explained to them that I had been photographing all day long at Pæstum, and the chemicals had stained my hands, and that if I had been a lord I should have had somebody to do it for me. One brigand said, "Look at his hands, they are black, indeed; his trousers (they were grey flannel), too, are like what prisoners wear, and they are all worn out, *povero uomo!*" The captain and the rest seemed rather disappointed, but said, "We will see; wait."

They offered us a little piece of hard sausage called *supersato*, but after discussing its digestible qualities together, we told them that it would not agree with us. They laughed, and the captain said, "They will like it by-and-by," which truly came to pass. I never heard the end of this; the brigands never forgot the two Englishmen discussing the wholesomeness of the sausage. We started again, passing by some men, an old woman, and two girls—the old woman was sent for water, which she brought in a broken fiasco. We were very thirsty, for it was a very hot day. We rested continually, Mr.

Aynsley always lying down at full length on his back. A little further on we found a spring, and here they filled a wide-awake and brought it to us. At last, about four o'clock, we reached the top of Monte Corvino, the highest mountain in the neighbourhood; a road ran along its base. We were placed under the shade of bushes close to a little spring: on the merits of this stream the brigands expatiated eloquently.

The captain asked me what I should like to eat. I answered like Sancho Panza, "Some meat, bread, wine, and eggs." He told me I should have them; but alas! like Sancho Panza, I was doomed to disappointment. For the next three days we had scarcely enough to keep body and soul together—only a mouthful each day of Indian corn bread. There was a goat tethered near us ready to be killed, and the remains of the fire, which they had left when they had descended from the mountains on their way to the plains.

The captain now got out paper and pen, and

commenced business. He took poor Luzzo in hand first. He was shivering with fear, and shrugging his shoulders when we looked at him. All the band began by raving at him, the captain shrieking at him and threatening him with all kinds of horrors, and told him that 12,000 ducats was his price. Manzo wrote a letter, which he gave me to read, but I told him he had only asked for twelve ducats, so I was requested to write it again for him, which I did. The other poor captive was now brought forward, 8000 ducats was his price; they both sat wringing their hands, declaring that such sums were quite out of their power to give. They met with nothing but ridicule and threats from the brigands.

It was now our turn, but there was at once a difficulty—" Whom to write to?" We said it was no use writing to our wives, they could do nothing in a foreign land. We had no money in Naples and no friends: one of us must go to get what money we could. When we heard the sum demanded,

we looked at each other with horror—100,000
ducats, equal to 17,000*l.* After a few minutes
conversation with Sentonio, a tall clumsy ruffian
with black eyes, hair, and beard, Manzo reduced it
to 50,000 ducats, or 8500*l.* This sum, we said,
was ridiculous, out of the question; but we were
told, in spite of our protestations to the contrary, that we had 2,000,000 ducats each, and that
we were great lords. We declared it was no
use to trust to our wives to raise the money, as
they did not speak the language, and that there
were few English people at Naples, and no one
would trust them as foreigners.

They then agreed to let one of us go for the
money, and wanted us to decide which it should
be; but we, knowing that whichever offered himself
would be kept back, were silent. At last we proposed
to draw lots, so I took a small twig and broke it
in two pieces, a short and a long piece, and we
arranged that the holder of the short one was to
remain with the band, and the holder of the

longer piece was to go and get the money for both. I took the pieces of wood, and holding out my hand before me, I said to Mr. Aynsley, "Draw." He drew one, and left the other (which was the shorter of the two) in my hand. I must confess I felt as if I had been drawing for my life, and I had lost.

I had to make up my mind to my fate at once. Mr. Aynsley told me he did not know whether he could pay so much. I told him that I could, and that I would advance his half for him till arrangements could be made. I told him to apply to a friend whom I named, a member of the Stock Exchange, for 2500*l.*, which I had left in his hands. I gave him other little directions, and told him to do all he could for my wife, placing her under his care. Our conversation was interrupted by the captain being called by the sentinel to come and look at about 100 soldiers walking along the road below. After a few minutes Mr. Aynsley and two men, to whom the letters of Luzzo and the other captive were given, were hurried away, Mr. Aynsley having to write to Luzzo's house.

I was put under the charge of four or five men, and ordered off to the rear. I turned round and saw Mr. Aynsley and his two guides walking down the hill. It was a trying moment. I was now driven on at a fast pace, and in a minute heard the report of a gun, the bullet whizzing over my head. This was from the soldiers whom Mr. Aynsley met almost immediately after leaving us. The brigands answered this, and there was a brisk fire. I tried to go off to the right, thinking an escape possible, but was turned immediately; my foot slipped, and I fell down some depth, for the mountain was very steep, and all the stones loose. I was very much shaken, and I thought my arm was broken. I could hardly move it, but I was made to get up, and to the cry " *Corre, corre,*" on we went.

The hill was very high, the base of it covered

with fir-trees. I looked up, and saw the rest of
the band lining the top of the hill in skirmishing
order, firing as fast as they could. The shots of the
soldiers now came rattling round us as we passed
from bush to bush one by one; and for a quarter
of an hour we had to run the gauntlet. At
last we got to the bottom of the mountain, where
we found a rushing torrent ten yards wide; the
fire was too hot for hesitation, so one by one the
brigands waded over. I had to follow; on I
went, the water up to my waist, rushing, foaming
over the stones, and the bullets splashing into it
on all sides of me. I do believe the soldiers
took special aim at me, the tallest of the party.
My death would no doubt have saved them considerable trouble. Had it not been for my stick,
I should have been carried away by the force of
the stream; as it was, I had to cross in an
oblique direction, landing on the other side only
two yards above a waterfall of some height. The
brigand who followed me was washed down, and

The Fight with the Soldiers on Monte Corrino.

went head over heels over the fall, but he was not much hurt, and scrambled out below. The others passed over safely, and we hurried up the steep ascent over the other side for some considerable distance till we were concealed among the trees, and safe from the fire of the troops. I thanked God for my escape from my rescuers, and felt anything but charitably disposed towards their rulers, who ought years ago to have cleared their country from these ruffians, instead of leaving them alone till they carried off an Englishman.

We rested among the trees until nightfall. At sunset we saw about two hundred soldiers in a body ascending the opposite bank by a path from the stream. They cheered as they marched along. I turned to the brigands and said, " You have lost some comrades." They did not choose to admit this. After dark some more shots were heard, and the band was surprised again. The other prisoners managed to escape—

lucky fellows—they were but small fry, and were forgotten in the excitement of the fight; but the greatest care was taken of me. I was never allowed a chance for a moment. When it was dark, we saw the bivouac-fire of the troops. We had no fire, but lay down under our capotes, I lying between two men. We soon forgot our fatigue in sleep, and an hour before sunrise I was woken up, stiff from the cold and wet, for the passage through the river had thoroughly soaked me. The walking, however, warmed us, and after an hour's march, by which time the day had dawned, we reached a spot hidden by broom, all golden with the yellow blossoms. It was a lovely place, the ground mossy, and covered with luxuriant creepers, graceful ferns, and foxgloves. Here we rested, a murmuring stream running below.

The ferns were at least ten feet high. I laid down and tried to sleep, but my thoughts would not allow me. I kept thinking of the desolate situation of my wife, and of the anxiety that would be felt by my family in England. I looked round for a chance of escaping, and edged off as far as I could from the men, but the slightest movement caused them to look after me with the cry *Che fate?* We were on the edge of a hill, at the base of which ran the rivulet, crossed by a rude bridge formed of the trunk of a tree. We saw soldiers passing at intervals all day in small bodies, eight or ten at a time, over the bridge and along a bridle-path near. It struck me that I might run off and cry out to the soldiers; but it was soon intimated to me by the brigands (they must have divined what was passing in my mind) that if I attempted to escape I should be shot at once. I noticed that the soldiers looked like mites, thus showing the great height of the mountain, and the distance we were from them. I now turned my attention to nearer objects, looking at the violets and forget-me-nots. I then read my prayer-book, which

I had found in my pocket. This was a great find, and afforded me the greatest comfort throughout my captivity. I read some of the Psalms, which brought tears to my eyes. The brigands soon perceived this, and entreated me not to be down-hearted, as they would not hurt me, if they got the money soon. I told them that it was not fear but grief for what my wife was suffering on my account. Talking, however, was not my humour then, and I would say no more to them, but returned to my sad meditations.

A little animal now came to make friends with me. I heard a slight rustle in some broom by my side. I looked round and saw the sleekest little mouse perched on the branch of a shrub of broom. It was of a fawn colour, with the brightest black eyes, and apparently very tame. As long as I looked at it it never moved, and only stirred when I put my hand near it, and then it only ran down the stem, but soon returned again. I felt very friendly to this little creature when I saw how beautifully and perfectly it was formed. I then thought of its Creator, who had called it into being, and who, as a benevolent Deity, had provided, as might be expected, for its nourishment. I drew consolation from this thought of God's care. My attention was drawn off from my little friend by the soldiers, and when I looked again he had gone, and did not return. I felt very hungry, for I had had no food since yesterday. I kept asking for bread, but was told that it was impossible to get any on account of the troops who were continually patrolling round us; but I kept asking all day, for I felt it was nothing to me what risk they ran in getting food. At last my friend Justi, who always pitied me, said he would go and try to get some. "There are kind hearts everywhere." He asked me if I had any money. I gave him a two-franc piece, but he said that was not enough, so I gave him five francs, and off he went. In about an hour he returned with something tied up in a cotton handkerchief, which proved to be Indian corn bread, broken in pieces. It seemed delicious for I was almost starving. I had no scruple about eating more than my share, and I put some into my pocket, but a very small portion, as the whole quantity brought was very little, and I was obliged to leave some for them. The old proverb is very true, "Hunger is the best sauce." No gourmand ever enjoyed his perigord pie as I did my dry crusts in the mountains. The flavour was exquisitely nice. It was now getting late in the afternoon, when some more soldiers passed. When once they were out of sight, we began to descend the mountain, keeping as much under cover as we could. I now saw how little chance I should ever have of escaping from the brigands. They ran down the mountain like goats, while I had to be careful to pick my way at every step. How could I hope to run away under these circumstances?

Accustomed to mountains from their earliest youth, they were as sure-footed as the goats, and had eyes like cats; darkness and light, daytime or night, made not the slightest difference to them. Their hearing, too, was most acute. This sense they had cultivated to such a pitch, that, like the red Indians, the slightest rustle of the leaves, the faintest sound, never escaped their notice. Men miles distant working in the fields, or mowing the grass, they could distinguish with the greatest ease. They knew generally who they were, young and old, and to what village they belonged; when I, perhaps, could barely distinguish living beings. They could describe all their motions. We crossed the stream again at dusk, and walked along the path lately traversed by the troops for some distance, and then turned off to the left, through a very thick wood, ascending for some hours. At last we reached the summit; the brigands now stopped, and there was hesitation and doubt in their manner. I could perceive that they did not know the road exactly. The direction we were pursuing— namely, N.W., would have led us to a sheer precipice. After a little consultation, a divergence to the westward was pronounced feasible. I declared it impossible; but, seeing two of them descend, I, for the honour of my country, followed.

It was so steep that we had to descend by aid of our hands, with our faces to the mountain— in fact, I turned myself from a biped into a four-legged animal. The old adage came to my mind, "You never know what you can do till you try." Without the assistance of the bushes and trees that grew there, it would have been impossible to descend. After a tiresome descent of an hour in the dark (for there was no moon), we reached the bottom. As far as I could make out, it was a curious, picturesque spot, the mountains rising all around, and on the south side a great square block of stone jutting out like a castle.

On the north-west side, the sloping side of the

mountain looked as if covered with snow. This effect proved to be produced by a kind of white limestone broken in small pieces. I put some in my pocket, but found after some time that specimens of geology and natural history were very inconvenient to carry, and they were all thrown away. By degrees, as our marches became more fatiguing, we walked over the broken limestone, and kept passing up and down hills, over most difficult and pathless places, where every spot had to be felt carefully by the foot before the weight of the body was trusted on it. I constantly trod on loose stones with my foot, and was in continual danger of spraining my ankle, as I walked on in the dark. It was "Mind your steps, sir," at every moment, and woe betide me if I did not. We continued this march until daybreak, when we rested and endeavoured to sleep. I found out, to my annoyance, that during this march I had lost a signet-ring I much valued. I had put it in my pocket for security, and this pocket had got torn in our scramble down the side of the mountain.

May 18.—I slept till eight or nine o'clock, and, on awaking and looking round, I found we were just above the dry bed of a stream that in winter ran down the mountain-side. We were facing the west, and at about half a mile off ran a stream like a delicate little silver serpent, twisting in and out of the bushes and green banks; on the other side of it was a bridle path. We saw several bodies of troops pass during the day, who were always watched with the greatest interest; and the merits of the different sorts of soldiers were freely discussed. I tried to get as far away from my guardians as I could, and then began to think over some plan of escaping. I propped up my straw hat on a peg, so that the men who were all below me might think I was sleeping; and then tried to edge off and to be ready for a run when more soldiers came; but one, who was very wary, and who turned out to be one of the four brigandesses, changed her position so as to see the place where I was.

The day seemed very long. I read my prayer-book. Seeing some "Forget-me-nots," they reminded me strongly of happy days in England, and, for want of anything better to amuse me, I picked one and fastened it in my prayer-book with a little piece of a postage-stamp I had in my pocket. Very curiously, without knowing it, I placed it just over the Gospel for the fifteenth Sunday after Trinity. Our Saviour there draws lessons from the flowers of the field. The little flower that I had plucked always afterwards spoke volumes to me in my solitude, and I drew intense comfort from the thought that God, who cares for the lilies of the field, would not forget me, and felt convinced that I should be saved in time; but I felt very wretched when I thought I might never again see those who were dear to me.

I was dreadfully hungry, and found in my pocket a piece of the Indian corn bread as large as a walnut; this soon went, and I turned out all my pockets, and discovered to my joy the little cabbage I had put away on the 15th. I ate that raw, and thought it anything but disgusting. I now found two roots of garlic: one satisfied me, the flavour being rather strong—(how soon I was cured of all daintiness! before I was with the brigands the smell of garlic alone was nauseous to me, let alone the taste)—the other I put again into my pocket. We had had some water to drink during the night, and with this I was obliged to be satisfied till the evening. A village was near, for we heard the bells of the church chiming the hours. I fancied we were near Castellamare; but, on asking one of the brigands if it were so, he replied "Yes," and I knew then at once that it could not be, for it is always the brigands' principle to deceive their captives as to where they are. At dusk we started again, finding it much further to the river than I imagined; the stream was full of water, and running down very fast. We stepped from stone to stone and got over dryfooted, followed the path some way, and then, as yesterday, diverged over mountains and through woods for four or five hours, till having reached an open part at the summit of a mountain covered with grass, there was a halt, and we lay down to sleep. The night was very cold, wet and foggy—in fact, we were actually in the clouds. Every night hitherto I had been allowed a *capote* to myself, but to-night some of the brigands growled at the cold, and one came to share my cloak with me. I did not approve of this, but I had to submit; the other three slept under another *capote*.

May 19.—We woke up an hour before daybreak, stiff from the cold; I could not move till I had rubbed my knees for ten minutes. We started again down-hill, and then along a path up another mountain. Walking by daylight for once in a way was a great treat to me, not only on account of the light, but also from having a path. As the sun got up we grew very thirsty, for we had only dared to stop half a minute for a drink the evening before, on account of the place being dangerous; and we had passed no streams during the night. After some time a search was made for snow, and at last, in a most unlikely place, under leaves, some was found. It was most delicious, and as we walked on I kept eating it. The brigands laid down on the ground and lapped up the water that had thawed, and was running among the decayed leaves. I thought of fever, and preferred the snow. Soon after this we passed a spring, where we stopped to rest and drink at about eleven o'clock.

I was here told that we were near the main body of the band, and on emerging from the trees we saw the captain and about twenty-five of his men reclining on the grass in a lovely glade, surrounded by large beech-trees, whose luxuriant branches swept the lawn. Several sheep and goats were tethered near, cropping the grass. The men, with their guns in their hands, their picturesque costumes and reclining postures, the lovely light and chequered shade of the trees, made a picture for Salvator Rosa. But I do not believe that Salvator Rosa, or any other man, ever paid a second visit to brigands, however great his love of the picturesque might be, for no one would willingly endure brigand life after one experience of it, or place himself a second time in such a perilous situation.

The band all rose, and looked very pleased at seeing me, for we had been separated from them since the fight on the 17th, and they were in great fear that I might have escaped, or have been rescued by the troops. I stepped forward and shook hands with the captain, for I considered it my best policy to appear cheerful and friendly with the chief of my captors. He met me cordially in a ready way, and asked me how I was. I said I was very tired and hungry, so he immediately sent one of his men off, who returned in a few minutes with a round loaf of bread, and another loaf with the inside cut out, and packed full of cold mutton cut into small pieces and cooked. I asked for salt, and was told it was salted. When cooked the meat tasted delicious to me, though it was awfully tough, for I had not had meat since luncheon on Monday, in the Temples of Pæstum, four days before. I ate a quantity, and then asked for water, which was brought to me in a large leathern flask, with a horn round the top and a hole on one side serving to admit air, as the water was required for drinking. I had observed a large lump of snow suspended by a stick through its centre, between two forked sticks; the water dripping from it was collected in flasks, and then drank. There were two or three of these flasks. The captain asked me if I was satisfied. I answered, "Yes."

I was then told that there were two more companions for me. I was taken through a gap in the trees to the rest of the band, about seventeen in number. Here I found those who were destined to be my companions for the next three weeks. A young man about twenty-eight, with a black beard of a month's growth, dressed just like Manzo's band, who was introduced to me as Don Cicc, *alias* Don Francesco Visconti, and one Tomasino, his cousin, a boy of fourteen years old. I shook hands with them, and condoled with them on our common fate, which Don Francesco described as fearful. I was told to sit down on one side, which I did, and looked around me.

The spot seemed perfect for concealment—we were at the top of a high mountain, entirely surrounded by high trees, excepting two small gaps serving for entrances, opposite to each other. The surface of the ground was quite level. About twenty yards away, on the side opposite to where I entered, there was a quantity of snow, from which

they cut the large pieces for drinking purposes.
I saw five or six men bringing a fresh block,
which they had just cut, and slung on a pole. It
was now a little before mid-day, and they were
preparing a cauldron full of *pasta* (a kind of
macaroni), which was ready by twelve o'clock.
Some was offered to me, which I accepted. One
brigand proposed putting the *pasta* into a hollow
loaf, but another brigand brought forward a deep
earthenware dish of a round shape. I thought
milk would be an improvement, so I asked for
some. Two men went to the goats and brought
some in a few minutes. The *pasta* was very
clean and well cooked. What with the meat
and bread, and this *pasta*, I made an excellent
dinner, and felt much better. The *pasta* was all
devoured in a few minutes by the band, who collected round the *caldaja*, and dipped in spoons
and fingers. I had now leisure to examine the
men: they were a fine, healthy set of fellows.

Here the two divisions of the band were

united, thirty men under the command of Gaetano Manzo, and twelve under Pepino Cerino. The latter had the two prisoners, who had been taken on the 16th April, near the village of Giffone, at five o'clock in the afternoon, as they were returning from arranging some affairs connected with the death of a relative.

The smaller band had four women with them, attired like the men, with their hair cut short—at first I took them for boys; and all these displayed a greater love of jewellery than the members of Manzo's band. They were decked out to do me honour, and one of them wore no less than twenty-four gold rings, of various sizes and stones, on her hands, at the same moment, others twenty, sixteen, ten, according to their wealth. To have but one gold chain attached to a watch was considered paltry and mean. Cerino and Manzo had bunches as thick as an arm suspended across the breasts of their waistcoats, with gorgeous brooches at each fastening. These were sewed on for security; little bunches of charms were also attached in conspicuous positions. I will now describe the uniforms of the two bands. Manzo's band had long jackets of strong brown cloth, the colour of withered leaves, with large pockets of a circular shape, on the two sides, and others in the breasts outside; and a slit on each side gave entrance to a large pocket that could hold anything in the back of the garment. I have seen a pair of trousers, two shirts, three or four pounds of bread, a bit of dirty bacon, cheese, &c., pulled out one after another when searching for some article that was missing. The waistcoats buttoned at the side, but had gilt buttons down the centre for show and ornament, the larger ones were stamped with dogs' heads, birds, &c. There were two large circular pockets at the lower part of the waistcoats, in which were kept spare cartridges, balls, gunpowder, knives, &c., and in the two smaller ones higher up; the watch on one side and percussion caps in the other. This garment was of dark blue cloth, like the trousers, which were cut in the ordinary way.

The uniform of Cerino's band was very similar, only that the jacket and trousers were alike of dark blue cloth and the waistcoat of bright green, with small round silver buttons placed close together. When the jackets were new they all had attached to the collars, by buttons, *capuces*, or hoods, which are drawn over the head at night or when the weather is very cold, but most of them had been lost in the woods. A belt, about three inches deep, divided by two partitions, to hold about fifty cartridges, completed the dress, which, when new, was very neat looking and serviceable. Some of the cartridges were murderous missiles. Tin was soldered round a ball so as to hold the powder, which was kept in by a plug of tow. When used the tow was taken out, and, after the powder was poured down the barrel, the case was reversed, and a lot of slugs being added, was rammed down with the tow on the top. These must be very destructive at close quarters, but they generally blaze at the soldiers, and *vice versâ*, at such a distance, that little harm is done from the uncertain aim taken. Most of them had revolvers, kept either in the belts or the left-hand pocket of their jackets; they were secured by a silk cord round their necks, and fastened to a ring in the butt of the pistol. Some few had stilettos, only used for human victims. Many wore ostrich feathers with turned up wide-awakes, which gave the wearers a theatrical and absurd appearance. Gay silk handkerchiefs round their necks and collars on their cotton shirts made them look quite dandies when these were clean, which was but seldom.

At last, tired of watching the band, I lay down and fell asleep. I slept for some hours, during which a poor sheep was dragged into the enclosure, killed, cut up, cooked in the pot, and eaten. I must have slept until near sunset, for when I awoke, another sheep was being brought forward, and I watched the process of killing and cutting up the poor beast. The sheep was taken in hand by two men, Generoso and Antonio generally acting as the butchers of the band. One doubled the fore-legs of the sheep across the head; the other held the head back, inserting a knife into the throat, and cutting the windpipe and jugular vein. It was then thrown down, and left to expire. When dead, a slit was made in one of the hind legs near the feet, and an iron ramrod taken and passed down the leg to the body of the animal; it was then withdrawn, and the mouth of one of the men placed to the slit in the leg, and the animal was inflated as much as possible and then skinned. When the skin was separated from the legs and sides, the carcase was taken and suspended on a peg on a tree, through the tendon of a hind leg; the skin was then drawn off the back (sometimes the head was skinned, but this rarely). The skin was now spread out on the ground to receive the meat, &c., when cut off the body; the inside was taken out, the entrails being drawn out carefully and cleaned; these were wound round the inside fat by two or three who were fond of this luxury; Sentonio, and Andrea the executioner, generally performing this operation. These delicacies, as they were considered, being made about four inches long, and about one inch in diameter, are fried in fat, or roasted on spits. It was some time before I could bring myself to eat these, but curiosity first, and hunger afterwards, often caused me to eat my share; for I soon learnt it was unwise to refuse anything.

While these two men were preparing the inside, the other two were cutting up the carcase. The breast was first cut off, and then the shoulders; the sheep was then cut in half with the axe, and then the bones were laid on a stump and cut through, so that it all could be cut in small pieces. One man would hold the meat, while another would take hold of a piece with his left hand and cut with his right. As it was cut up, the pieces would be put into a large cotton handkerchief, which was spread out on the ground; the liver and lungs were cut up in the same way; the fat was then put in the *caldaja*, and, when this was melted, the kidneys and heart (if the latter had not been appropriated by some one) were roasted on spits, and eaten; everyone helping himself by dipping his fingers in the pot. The pieces of liver were considered the prizes. All the rest of the sheep was then put in the pot at once, and after a short time the pot was taken off the fire and jerked, so as to bring the under pieces to the top.

They liked the meat well cooked; and when once pronounced done, it was divided into as many equal portions as there were numbers present; the captives being treated as " companions"—the term they always used in speaking of one another—I soon found that the sooner I picked up my share the better. If there was no doubt about there being plenty for all, the food was never divided. Then they dived with their hands, whoever ate fastest coming off best. I could only eat slowly, having to cut all the meat into shreds, as it was so tough; so I always took as much as they would let me, and retired to my lair, like a dog with his bone. If I finished this before all was gone, I returned for more—it being always necessary to secure as much as possible, as one was never sure when more food would be forthcoming, and it is contrary to brigand etiquette to pocket food when eaten thus. When it was divided, I might of course do as I liked with my share, but even then it was prudent not to allow them to know that I had reserved a stock in my pocket, or I was sure to come off short on the next division taking place. The skin was now taken and stretched out to dry, and then used to sleep on. I now had a talk with Visconti, who told me he had been with the brigands more than a month, having been taken by Pepino's band of twelve men, close to his house in Giffone, with his little cousin, Tomasino. 40,000 ducats was the price asked for him, of which 9000 had already been paid. He complained wofully of the life and the scarcity of food, though he had never really suffered from want, the band having laid their hands on twenty sheep at once while he was with them. The length of the days troubled him much. He had not had much walking, and had been eight days in the present encampment. He had suffered from fever for some days, but was now better. He looked very white and puffy in the face. Little Tomasino was as fat as possible, and seemed to enjoy his life like a child, not reflecting on the danger of his situation. He was a great favourite with the band, and was already half a brigand. While talking, we were startled by an accidental shot from one of the brigand's guns; this made a great stir among the band, and called down the severe displeasure of the captain, who scolded the delinquent most warmly. It now grew dark, and the captain came round and told me to lie down on two sheep-skins which had been assigned to me. A wallet was given me for a pillow, and also a *capote*. I was very tired, notwithstanding my sleep in the afternoon, and soon fell asleep. The captain and ten or twelve men went down the mountain in the meantime to watch. About eleven o'clock we were awakened by firing, and there was soon a volley, by which we knew they had fallen in with the troops. After a time all was quiet again, and towards the morning the captain returned with the news that one of the men had been shot while carrying bread and honey in a handkerchief on his gun over his shoulder. He fell immediately. (Signor D—— afterwards told me that it was his act.) There was great lamentation; and, at an hour before sunrise, the whole band was collected, and started off in flight.

On the 20th we did not march very far, only walking about two hours in the shade of the wood till we got lower down, where we rested for the day. A great deal of gambling went on all day long. Pepino's band were the players, for they had lately received 9000 ducats of Visconti's ransom. Their game was something of this sort: three or four men sat round a handkerchief spread on the ground; three half napoleons were then put into a wide-awake, the lining being first torn out. The hat was then shaken, and turned over, so as to drop out the coins which were then concealed by the hat. Money is now staked on the *croce* or *capo*. All day long it was a perpetual " *cinque a cinque capo, vint' a vinte,*" and so on. I was always apprehensive of danger when the gambling was going on, for after a few minutes there was sure to be a quarrel, and when their passions were roused they were always more inclined to treat me badly. Loud voices would be heard, those making the greatest noise demanding silence, and the captain, who was as inveterate a gambler as any of them, would storm and rage at his men in the most furious manner. The gambling would often be carried on in the most dangerous places, even when the soldiers were known to be near, and when the risk attending a quarrel among themselves might easily have been fatal to the brigands.*

No fire was made to-day on account of the proximity of the soldiers, who disturbed the band last night. Bread in small quantities was divided amongst us, but there was no water. Two hours before sunset we started again, there being great groans from Visconti and many of the band on account of the long walk before us—seven or eight hours' march; for, though always walking, the brigands dislike and dread much of it. Soon after starting, it began to rain hard. I turned

---

* "It is worthy the observing, that there is no passion in the mind of man so weak but it mates and masters the fear of death."—*Bacon's Essays.*

my flannel trousers up to my knees, and put on my *capote*, thinking it better to endure a little cold than get my trousers wet. This horrified the brigands, who were most anxious that I should put them down again, saying that it was very injurious to expose the knees. I told them it was the Scotch fashion, and Scotland had plenty of rain, and the people were renowned for their courage, strength, and good sense. The grass and trees were very wet, and our boots and socks were soon wet through. In a short time we left the wood, and falling on a path, we pursued our way with the greatest caution, the captain being always in advance and the others following in Indian file. The captives had to march towards the rear with about four or five men behind them; one man, Pavone by name, being especially charged to take care of me. He was responsible for me, and if I had escaped his life would have been forfeited. Another, called Scope,* who was also charged never to leave me,

* Abbreviated from Scopecchia.

was behind me. These two never left me, day or night. Scopo, with two others, came from Acerno, and had only joined the band a few days before we were captured. He had been a *zappadore*, or labourer in the fields; his nature was most brutal. He was always with me, and invariably ill treated me. He grudged me every morsel I had to eat, and whenever he gave me any food he always threw me my portion, as if I had been a dog. He was a tall, spare man, about twenty-two years old, with a long thin face, with large nose and large eyes. His eyes had always a mournful expression, and were constantly fixed on the ground. Remorse for some fearful deed of murder was clearly written on his countenance, as though he were already suffering for it. I often used to charge him with thinking of his victim, but he would never admit it—a shake of the forefinger or contemptuous tap on the head being all the answer he would deign to give me. We now came to a long stripe of open ground, the forest of large beech-trees skirting it on the left, and the mountain, with a gentle slope, rising on the right. Some of this ground was cultivated, and had just been ploughed and sown with maize, or *granone*, as they call it. We were cautioned against speaking, or walking on the soft ground, and were told to tread upon the grass, so that we might not leave any traces to betray our track to the troops, or to any of that class called by the brigands *infame*—the term they use for informers, and all those who are not well-disposed towards them, and would give any notice or information to the authorities. After walking some hours' time we passed several *pagliatte* or straw conical huts. Some little distance from us there was a light in the last of these, arising from a wood fire in front. We were halted while some of the advance guard went up to reconnoitre. One brigand went forward to speak to the occupants, who proved to be shepherds; they had put out the fire as the band approached, and after a short conversation the two shepherds were brought down to the captain, who had remained with the band under a large spreading oak-tree. I stepped forward, longing to see an honest face, but was roughly pulled back, and told to stop where I was. My blood boiled for a moment, but I restrained myself, and endeavoured to show indifference by a shrug of the shoulders. It was their invariable practice to prevent their captives from seeing or speaking to the peasants. I inquired why this was so, and was told that the peasants object to it, for fear of being recognised and denounced afterwards when the prisoner has been ransomed and is free. The captain asked me if I should like some milk. I cheered up a little at the prospect of a drink at last, and a large pailful having been brought to me I took it in my hands, and did not take it from my lips till I felt I had had enough. This was the first opportunity they had of observing my milk-consuming powers. They were rather astonished, and I explained that "*Latte me piace molto,*" as it did all English people. I did not know when I should have a chance of drinking again, and acted on Captain Dugald Dalgetty's plan of laying in a stock when I had the opportunity. The two Viscontis hardly drank any, being of opinion that it was unwholesome; they are like their countrymen; they rarely touched milk. (In Rome it is a common sight to see written in English, "Milk sold here," English people being the principal consumers of that beverage.) After a halt of about half-an-hour, we continued our walk. Pavone asked me if I knew where Salerno was, and was annoyed at my pointing without any hesitation towards it. Then followed a question as to where Pæstum (or Peste, as they call it,) was. I pointed correctly as before, and also showed them the directions in which lay Rome, Apulia, and, lastly, England. They did not know the north star, which was now shining brightly, the rain having left off and the sky being quite clear; and my knowing the way, as they said, always, both by day or night, in any part of the mountains, puzzled them immensely. They never got over it, continually asking me throughout my captivity how it was that I obtained this wonderful knowledge.

On this particular occasion my extraordinary cleverness, as they termed it, was their topic of conversation all night. The ground we were now traversing was more cultivated, and we passed another river, the Viscontis and I being carried across on the shoulders of some of the band. The path then grew better and ran between hedges. It was now very dark, and I had great difficulty in following, not being able to see an inch before me, and I was obliged to take hold of the man walking before me, and to feel every step before I ventured to put my foot to the ground. Sometimes I lagged a little, and those behind now and then gave me a rap, and were in a great rage with me, Pavone indulging in a few oaths at the same time. After five hours' walking our captors began to get very tired, and poor Visconti was very foot-sore. I fortunately had a pair of well-fitting strong boots on, and, excepting that my right ankle felt a little warm, I was well enough, and ready to walk on for some hours more. I inquired how much longer we should be walking. Some said half an hour, others four or five hours; the good-natured ones of the band always shortening the time to encourage us, the others doing the reverse. It was almost an impossibility for them to tell the truth at any time, on any subject. Another hour brought us to a place where our approach disturbed some dogs, which barked most furiously till we were again far away from them. We were now told that we were getting near our sleeping-place; the district got more wild and rocky, and we heard the rushing sound of a mountain torrent, and, after following it some little way, we came to a place with rocks rising on each side; the river running between them, and leaving a small level space between it and the rocks on one side.

CHAPTER VI.

THE CAPTIVE'S DIARY CONTINUED: MAY 20 TO 27.

Brigands merry-making—The Captain watches over me while I sleep—His protecting Care—Thoughts of Home—A Storm—The Ladies of the Band—Doniella—Carmina—Marie—Antonina—Concetta—Their Furniture—They think I am a Milord—The Government will pay for me—A Night March—A terrific Climb—Method of selecting Sentries—Threats of Mutilation.

CHAPTER VI.

May 20.—The edge of the stream was fringed with bushes, two or three trees growing by the side of the rocks on the right of the level ground. As soon as we arrived at the camping-ground, the band gave themselves up to mirth and merriment, as they always did on coming to any place where they considered themselves perfectly safe. This encampment being below the level of the surrounding country, and the noise of the turbulent stream drowning the sound of their voices, made them now feel themselves quite secure. All but two or three burst out into one of their favourite songs; the others set to work to collect dead wood for the fire, and to cut a curved branch, which was driven into the ground near the fire, and on which was suspended the *caldaja* or caldron, containing one of the sheep that were killed when we left the top of the mountain in the morning. The fire soon burnt up; a quantity of wood was piled on, and we all crowded round to warm and dry ourselves, it having rained so heavily during our night's march. The favourite song of the band was now sung by all, and the light shining on those standing and sitting round the fire, as well as lighting up the little amphitheatre, made the whole scene most picturesque. I walked two or three steps to the river, in order to bathe my right ankle, which felt a little warm. Immediately there was a cry of *"Dove andate?"* and it was with some difficulty that I persuaded those who came to look after me to allow me to put my foot into the icy cold water. They tried to persuade me that it was most injurious, and that I should do myself some serious harm, and they eventually made me come back to the fire, long before I had had time enough to bathe my foot.

In a few minutes the meat was cooked enough to please them, and divided into forty-five parts upon one of the *capotes*; three parts were given to the captives, the others coming forward to take their share. All the bread had been eaten during the day, so that we had to devour the lumps of tough mutton alone. Two other fires were now lighted up, and I tried to dry my *capote* and boots as much as possible, but in a few minutes I was shown the place allotted to me for the few hours that remained before sunrise.

The two Viscontis and I lay down together. I was on the outside, with the captain close to me. To make doubly-sure he put one leg over my chest; I tried to shake it off, but he would have it so; and, being very tired, I tried to forget all, and was soon asleep.

May 21.—It seemed only five minutes when I was roused up, hearing a stern voice say "*Alza!*" which is their word for "get up." There was no denying them, so up I got, grieving over our fate at having to start again, for I had hoped, and fully expected, that we should have stopped some time at this place. We climbed up the rocky bank, and soon began to ascend a mountain covered with beech trees, the branches of which we had to bend on one side, in order to make our way through them. A tremendous thunderstorm now broke over us, with drenching rain, and after getting thoroughly wet, we reached a grotto where we rested. Here I heard, to my horror, that the two poor proprietors whom we had seen captured by the brigands, and who had been our companions during the first night's walk and the next day till the attack of the soldiers, had been murdered on that occasion when trying to escape. (I afterwards found out that this was not true. Luzzo had complained of the cold on the evening of the 15th, and Manzo generously lent him his own jacket. This Luzzo had on when he escaped, and in it was a pocket-book containing papers, some of which were accounts of large sums of money expended for the band, while others were said to compromise certain neighbouring proprietors.) This filled me with anguish and anxiety as regarded my poor wife; for if she had heard that some of the *ricattati* had been killed, she would at once fear for me. I asked Manzo where Luzzo was, in order to be certain whether what I had heard was true: for one of the principles of brigandage is never to tell the truth, and the only way to ascertain anything, was to ask several of my captors the same question, when I had an opportunity of doing so alone, without the others hearing me; and then from the various answers, I would glean an approximation to the truth. Sometimes six or seven of them would give me quite different answers. The reply I got from the captain was "*Non c'è*," and that my letters and money were not to be sent to Luzzo's house, but that other arrangements had been made. He took paper out of his pocket-book, and un-

screwed a little black tin inkbottle, in which was
steel pen and some cotton waste; a little water
was added to this and stirred up; the water now
became black and served for ink; a large flat
round loaf was brought me to write on, and the
captain began to dictate a letter for me to write
to our Consul-General at Naples. The composi-
tion went on very slowly, by reason of my having
had very little practice in writing Italian, and
the Neapolitan dialect being so unlike the Roman,
which is always spoken by Englishmen.

When this was done, the letter to my wife,
which I had written on the 19th, at the place
where I joined the band, was given back to me,
to add a postscript, stating that all letters and
money were to be sent to the house of my fellow-
sufferer's father at Giffone.

At twelve o'clock noon, some *pasta* was cooked,
which, with a little bread, and still less raw
fat bacon, constituted our dinner. I now remembered that to-day was Sunday, and I thought

of home, and the many happy Sundays we had spent there; and of the little church, where I felt that many silent prayers were being offered up on my behalf; (and where, as I afterwards learnt, I was prayed for by name, all those weary months that I remained in the hands of my captors.) I read all our beautiful church service; how different it appeared to me now in my lonely and terrible position to what it did when read in churches—the prayers and psalms seemed as though written *for me!* What confidence and trust they gave me, that by the grace of God I should be delivered from the hands of those wicked men! From this day till I was set free, I never missed reading through the whole of the morning service and litany. I generally chose the afternoon about two o'clock, when the band, (like all southerners) with the exception of the sentries, all slept, and thus gave me a quiet interval from the swearing, gambling, and disputing, that were always going on around me.

At about two o'clock the captain and ten of the band went off with my letters; and the others with us climbed higher up the mountain. Soon after starting the sky grew very dark, with every appearance of another storm, which fortunately did not break until we were under the shelter of a grotto—about an hour's walk from where we had spent the morning. The grotto was very small, and only afforded room sufficient for Visconti and myself, little Tomasino creeping in behind us. About five or six feet in front of the cave was a large heap of snow that had remained unmelted in consequence of a quantity of earth having fallen upon it from the rocks above. I was about to eat some, but they would not allow me because of the earth over it, which they said generally made the snow injurious by means of poisonous matter washed from it. The cave was very damp, and the sides covered with green mould; the part between it and the bank of snow was very uneven and sloping, so Sentonio (who, though the oldest, yet was always the most active of the band) borrowed my stick, and with the point of it, dug up the upper part, and in a short time made a level space large enough to accommodate the brigands with us. The storm now broke, accompanied by a most furious shower of rain that lasted about half an hour, after which it became fine again. This was the sort of weather we had for at least six weeks, though all the time it was fine and without a drop of rain in the plains of Naples and Salerno. Towards the evening a larger and drier grotto was discovered by those who went for water, a little lower down on the right; so we were moved to it after some hesitation on the part of Sentonio, who had worked so hard in order to level the ground; and we soon got wet again. How I hated these changes after we had settled down quietly! Three fires were, however, lighted on arriving at our new place of shelter, and we did our best to dry our boots and *capotes*. Our supper consisted of *pasta* again. The captain and men came back during the night with bread, some large sugar-plums, which they call *confetti*, and two bottles of *Rosolio*, which is a sort of sweetened rum. The captives had a share of these, and we thoroughly enjoyed them, having been without any luxury of the kind for a week.

May 22.—To-day we had a repetition of the wet and thunder of yesterday, and to my horror we went down to the glen where we were yesterday morning, thus wetting my boots through again.

Here I discovered that five of the band were *brigandesses*. They were dressed exactly like the men, and their hair was cut short, the only peculiarity in their clothing being small boneless articles, which, I believe, ladies call corsets. They exhibited none of that sanguinary and savage character which I had always heard belonged to lady-brigands; all four were part of the goods and chattels of their respective masters.

They were considered by all as the *ultime compagne* of the band; they had no share in the ransom money, and were often beaten and ill-treated by their lords. Two of them carried guns, and the other three revolvers. Two were tall, fine, strong young women; the third had a melancholy thin face, but the largest oval eyes I had ever seen; the fourth was an ugly, sulky girl, who always appeared to refuse food or anything offered to her, and the fifth was very much like her.

Doniella, the partner of Pepino Cerino, the *capo* of the small band of eleven men, who had taken Don Francesco and his cousin Tomasino, was a strapping young woman of about nineteen years old, with a very good figure and handsome features, a pretty smile and splendid teeth. She and her husband were both very greedy, and always managed to secure a double share of food, which made them very unpopular, and was eventually the cause of Pepino being deposed from his office of captain. She would sometimes give us *confetti*, but always refused us any of the extra share of food which she always had in her pocket. I often wondered how it was that she was generous enough to give me a *capuce* or hood, of blue cloth, which she did during our night's march of the 19th; but after six weeks I found out that it belonged to Cerino, who, to my grief, came to claim it when his band parted from Manzo's. This *capuce* was the greatest comfort at night. I always tied a cotton handkerchief, which they gave me, round my head, and then drew on this hood of double cloth half over my face, keeping off all wind and wet.

Carmina belonged to Giuseppe, a good-looking man, with red fuzzy hair of prodigious length; he was the dandy of the band, and had the reputation of being rich, that is, of possessing 4000 ducats. Many were the rings and gold chains on their persons and in their pockets, for a *festa* or some grand occasion was necessary to draw out of the little tin boxes that served them for jewel cases the wealth they contained. Carmina was very good-natured, and would nearly always give me any food she could spare.

Maria was the sulky girl. She hardly ever spoke to anybody, and when any one addressed her, a nod or shake of the head was all the response she would deign to give; she would never give me anything, or do anything for me.

Antonina was the lotus-eyed damsel. She possessed a cheerful disposition, and was always willing to do anything she could for me in the mending way. She attached herself to Generoso Saliverra, who fully carried out the import of his name. Many a time when food was very scarce would these two share with me the little that they had saved from the previous day. I considered that all was fair in war, and never lost an opportunity of securing whatever I could lay my hands on. Many a time I endeavoured to impress on them that, as an Englishman, I required double the quantity that would suffice for them; but I regret to say that this had little effect, except in giving them the idea that I had an insatiable appetite.

Concetta belonged to Cicco Guange, and was very similar in disposition to Maria.

All these women had about them, needles, scissors, cotton and silk of various hues, as well as bits of cloth, and they were always ready to do any repairs that were needful; and when a fresh supply of handkerchiefs (or *maccatore*, as they were termed) arrived, they would all sit together and steadily work away till they were done. During a thunderstorm they would always cease working—out of some religious feeling—and at every clap of thunder cross themselves. Sunday was the same as other days as regarded working. I tried to explain to them that they should rest from labour on that day, but always without effect.

On the western side of this glen, in which we

remained all day, there was a high bank of earth
with the roots of the large beech-trees protruding
from it. In the winter the glen served as a
watercourse; but it was now quite dry, and
served as a capital place of concealment, though
on that account it was all the worse for us.
The dense forest of beech-trees that clothed the
whole side of the mountain prevented us seeing
beyond a very little way, and the ground was
everywhere covered with dead leaves, six inches
deep, packed closely together by the weight of
the snow in winter.

I looked round to discover something that
might perchance serve to pass away the weary
hours; flowers there were none, but suddenly my
eye rested on a twisted root, about five inches
thick. It struck me that I might be able to
manufacture a spoon, to be my own, so that it
would not be necessary to use one that had just
been in the mouth of a murderer. I got up,
took the hatchet, and began with gentle and silent

strokes to cut a piece about six inches long; three or four of my guardians soon inquired what I was doing, and told me not to make a noise. After five minutes Pavone came up, and with two or three cuts, much more violent than I had dared to make, separated the desired piece. They asked what I wanted it for, and were much amused when I told them that it was for the purpose of making a spoon. This kept me amused for two whole days; hour by hour I perseveringly kept whittling away with a tiny little penknife, one and a quarter inches long, with a most delicate little blade of the best steel I ever saw. Many a day did that precious little knife amuse me, and many a time did I refuse to lend it for fear it should come to grief. Sometimes I was obliged to do so, but then I never rested till it was again safe in my possession.

It was very cold at night, and the ground being very wet on account of the constant storms and rain, I always tried to dry my *capote* as much as I could, but the thick woollen cloth absorbed so much water that I could never do so perfectly, and I always woke in the morning shivering with cold, and with my joints quite stiff. I rubbed my knees for some time and then tried to get close to the fire, which was always made at daybreak to thaw us, for many of the band were without *capotes*, having lost them on the 16th, when surprised by the troops. Some of the men would not let me go near the fire until they were forced to do so by those well-disposed towards me. When warm, or a little less cold, I would try to go to sleep again till about eight o'clock, when we would eat what little was given to us, generally at this time a little piece of very hard stale bread, about three inches square.

May 23.—Repetition of yesterday.

May 24.—Great rain to-day. Early in the

morning we were sent to the cave above, where we had spent the 21st; we got very wet, and had to lie in our wet things all day. In the afternoon there was another frightful storm; all the brigands crossed themselves as peal succeeded peal of thunder. Towards the evening it was fine again, and after sunset the four men who had been out foraging returned with a little bread and cheese.

May 25.—To-day was very quiet, Visconti and I talking to each other continually. Through disuse of my own language, I found Italian much more easy than at first, and we got on very well together. I asked him about country life in Italy, and he, in return, of mine in England. He, as well as the brigands, would have it that I was "My lord," and that wretched little Tomasino would come up to me and tell me that, from certain information the brigands had got, I was possessed of 2,000,000 ducats, and that the

Italian Government was going to pay my ransom, in which case they would not be contented with the 50,000 asked, but would not let me go under 1,000,000. This enraged me immensely, and I am afraid I sometimes was very unkind to the poor little fellow.

To-day Visconti most generously gave me a thick flannel sleeve-waistcoat, as he had two of these articles. It was most acceptable to me, because I was most miserably clothed, my dress being only suited to the hot plains. I do not know how I should have got on without this extra garment. In the middle of the day some of the band arrived with two sheep. I rejoiced to see them, for we had not had any meat for five or six days. The sheep were soon killed, skinned, and in the great camp kettle; but Visconti and I were horrified at finding we had to eat the meat without bread. I had secured a heart, which I roasted on a stick, and divided with Visconti, as I always did with anything that I could secure apart from the general division. On searching in my pocket I found a little piece of bread, which I had put away and forgotten; this I ate as dessert, in order to take away the taste of meat. We were told not to eat all, but to reserve some for the evening. But now a difficulty arose with us as regarded carrying it. The cleanest thing we could produce was my white pocket-handkerchief. There was no help for it—I had to sacrifice it; and wrapping up our joint store, I put it in the left pocket of my coat, which from this time served as my larder. An hour before sunset everything was packed away, and we were informed that a long march was before us. I was very cold, and a biting wind was blowing, so that I was rather rejoiced than otherwise, for I dreaded sleeping in the open air these damp cold nights. I always dreaded, too, waking up in the morning, on account of the piercing cold—dreaming, perchance, of home, and then suddenly finding myself in the midst of these ruffians.

It was a long up-hill walk through the forest; we rested once for an hour, and then started off again in Indian file. It was very dark, and again I had the greatest difficulty in following. I found the best plan was to grasp with my left hand the shoulder or muzzle of the gun of the man before me. As we approached the summit of the mountain, the force of the wind and the cold increased. Several of those in front went on, while we were halted and told to lie down, as the tops of the mountains were always considered dangerous, for the soldiers are often stationed there, and make *baraques*, or round huts, of fresh-cut boughs, in which they pass the nights. With what envy I passed these! I looked on them as palaces, and always asked the brigands why they did not use them, but a shake of the forefinger was the invariable reply. After reconnoitring some way in advance, a low whistle informed us that all was right. We were told to rise, and a few steps took us to the top.

May 26.—On looking about, I found that we were on the summit of a very high mountain (Monte Polveracchio). Morning was beginning to dawn, and I could perceive mountains all round us. In the distance, towards the west, I fancied I saw the sea, which proved to be the case. When it grew more light, towards the north-west I perceived the outline of the mountains at the back of Salerno, and stretching out to sea was the part beyond Vietri. I felt too miserable to look longer in that direction, the idea of actually seeing the place where my dear wife probably was, being too much for me. Fortunately, the march now required all my attention; it was along the sharp edge of the summit, and in many places a false step on either side would have been attended with great danger, for, on account of the precipices on each side, every step had to be taken with care and judgment, the more so because of the furious wind which threatened often to blow me over the edge. When we had gone some way along this narrow part, I perceived a town below us, on a small and perfectly level plain, one end of which was covered with large chestnut-trees. This, Visconti told me, was Acerno, a place which afterwards became of great importance to me, as I was eventually set free when in the immediate neighbourhood of it.

We now turned off towards the right down a very steep descent; I slipped and fell, the captain seeing which told one of the band to carry my *capote*, which I was carrying on my back, rolled up and slung with a piece of cord. I was delighted at being eased of my burden, and was able to walk much more easily; my feet were now in capital walking order, and my boots, though by no means new, still in fair condition, and were stout, and fitted me well. This was a great comfort, for it was heart-breaking to see poor Don Francesco, who suffered dreadfully from blisters at his heels, his feet being, as he expressed it, " *Tutti consumati.*"

Little Tomasino walked capitally for a boy, but he and Visconti were both constantly being urged on by the brigands. I always walked in front of them, and found no difficulty in keeping up at their pace. After having descended for about three quarters of an hour, we saw a frightful precipice rising perpendicularly on our left, and a deep ravine below us. It was necessary to cross the ravine; but the opposite side was very perpendicular, and the rock very loose and rotten. A halt was called while three or four descended to see whether it was practicable to ascend the other side. When they reached the bottom we watched them in order to know if we should follow, but as soon as they got up a yard or so the rock broke away, and down they slid again; at last, after about an hour, we saw one of them appear on the large rock that jutted out at the top of the precipice on our left, about 500 feet higher than where we were. He called out to us and we answered. We were horrified with the idea of having to follow to that inaccessible crag. I never saw a place more fitted for an eagle's nest. All those below had found it impossible to follow Luigi in scaling the crumbling rock, his very ascent having made it impracticable for those below him. He sat down contentedly, and watched us below. After a short time, we heard a call from the face of the precipice. We looked round and saw two of the others clinging on to the face of it, and slowly creeping, without their shoes, along its surface. At one spot where they stopped, the little ledge, three or four inches wide, on which they had passed, came to an end, and there was an interval of four or five feet without an atom of support to the foot. Luigi saw the difficulty; he descended to them, and, stretching out his arms, helped the foremost one to pass. This was done successfully, after some minutes' attempt, and when the others saw him safe they all gave a little kind of cheer. I declared it impossible to reach the place, for I saw no fun in risking my neck for these wretches; and poor Visconti kept appealing to heaven. All those with us looked very blue; but, after the second man had passed safely, the captain stepped forward and got over all right. The three now looked like a little flock of goats, feeling as happy at having passed safely as we felt miserable at the prospect of doing so.

I did not like the idea of being outdone by these men, so I volunteered to go next. I found mere little knobs of rock jutting out. Step by step I progressed, without daring to take my eyes off my feet and the inequalities in the surface, to which I clung with my hands. It was a fearful place. I stopped for a moment to survey my position above. The rock was 500 feet high, and below there was a sheer descent of 800 to 1000 feet. I am fortunate enough to possess rather a hard head, not given to dizziness, but I confess my position gave me rather a twist for a moment. However, the thought that the other three had passed gave me courage, and on I crept. At last I arrived at the gap. One of those that had passed came to help me. I stretched my right leg as far as I could, and, with a spring, over I went, and, with a lighter heart, went gaily up the now comparatively easy ascent to the crag. One by one they all came over. Poor Visconti was helped all the way, and when he reached us he was still uttering his pious ejaculations, with his hands raised towards heaven. We now went over the top, and descended among some enormous beeches where the woodcutters had been at work, leaving innumerable chips covering the ground. A little farther on we halted for the day, and Luigi, an old brigand belonging to Cerino's band, began to cut at a great piece of beech-wood with the axe. When he had got it about an inch thick, I asked him what he was going to do with it, and he told me that he was going to make a ramrod for a man called Rocco, who had broken the one belonging to his gun. Thinking it would amuse me for an hour or two to make it, I volunteered to do so, and Luigi handed the stick over to me, my skill at spoon-making having caused me to be considered *talented*, as they expressed it. It amused them much to see my way of going to work. I rested one end against my chest and the other in a notch, which I cut in a tree with the axe, and then, taking one of their murderous knives by the handle and point, I sliced little pieces off till it was about the size required. All the band collected round me, watching me with admiring eyes. After scraping it a little with some glass from a bottle broken on purpose, and greasing it with a little piece of fat bacon, it was pronounced perfect. I was rather proud of my work. It was quite straight and round, and fitted the gun capitally.

When it was done, a bright thought struck me. I asked them what it would cost in a town. "A ducat," was the answer. Then I said, "It was surely worth two ducats in the woods." "*Sicuro*," was the reply all round. "Then give me half a *marengo*," I burst out; "I do not see why you should not pay me as well as a gunmaker." Pepino, the *capo*, said nothing, but all the rest burst out laughing for a quarter of an hour. I kept demanding it, saying, "*Datemi il denaro;*" and, at last, Pepino drew out half a napoleon and handed it over to me! I told them I should have "*La Banda di Manzo*" cut on it, and that I should wear it on my watch-chain. This delighted them immensely, and they were good-tempered with me all that day, though there was a great lack of food, and we were reduced to eating the crumbs and dirt at the bottom of our pockets, which were always afterwards reserved for such occasions.

An hour before sunset we started again, passing through the dense forest, ascending all the time till we reached the summit of the mountain. Here we rested till it grew dark, when we began to descend the open grassy side facing the south-west, leaving the woods behind us on the northern slopes. This was generally the case with all the mountains, the north side getting less of the hot burning sun, and thus retaining more of the moisture, so necessary for forest-trees.

After a descent of 400 or 500 feet, we came to a shallow ravine with a thicket of trees, which was to be a halting-place for the night. They then proceeded to select the sentinels for the night. This was done as follows:—

All the band, except the women and those that were ill, stand up and form a circle, and then, at a signal from the captain, throw out their right hands, with various numbers of fingers extended, in the same way as the national game of "*La Morra*" is played. The captain, now inside the circle, walks round and counts the fingers extended, and then, retaking his place, counts from himself all round the circle, and the unlucky man on whom the number falls, together with his neighbours, have to commence the watch. Three hours is the usual time.

I often used to offer to take my turn, especially when only one sentinel was necessary, but I was always refused with laughter and thanks. We went supperless to bed: that is, we lay down on the damp ground, Don Francesco and I under one *capote*, for his had been taken away by one of the band, they considering that one *capote* was plenty for two. There was always a debate how it was to be arranged, Visconti wanting it to be all above us, but I being firm in having a little piece underneath; so we spread it over and then tucked in the sides underneath to lie upon; but, if either turned, it reduced the other to grief. Many were the growls this occasioned, for the wet soon made itself felt unless the cloak was well under us, and I always dreamt of rheumatism.

May 27.—We all woke up this morning very cold and stiff. Little fires were lighted as usual, but here great caution was requisite because of our exposed position, and many were the ravings directed against those warming themselves, on account of more smoke rising than was considered prudent. They were all particularly savage this morning, as food was wanting, and this always excited their ire against the unfortunate captives, and at the present time against me in particular, for no letters or money had been received from my friends. For a long time they kept surrounding me, pointing guns, revolvers, and knives at me, explaining to me which were the most delicate parts of the body, and how life was the most easily taken.

I always made it a point to appear perfectly unmoved on these occasions. My invariable phrase was, "*Se volete,*" implying that they were perfectly at liberty to take my life, and that in doing so would save my friends and myself a great deal of trouble and loss of money, and that I was quite sure that they cared more for my money than for taking my life. After a short time I found that my perfect indifference rather amused them, and "*Se volete*" became by-words of the band for everything whereby indifference was implied. We had very little food the last two days, but to-day there was nothing whatever, and I grumbled immensely, telling them that Englishmen always eat double the amount of food that Italians are satisfied with. Poor Visconti wrung his hands, perpetually saying "*Terribile ! Terribile !*" Supperless we lay down last night, supperless we did the same to-night, trying to make the best of it, and hoping for better luck the next day.

CHAPTER VII.

THE CAPTIVE'S DIARY CONTINUED.

MAY 28.

The Second Sunday—Good News for Visconti—More Letter-writing—An Attempt at Sketching—The Englishman's Appetite—Alarms—The Soldiers—A Tradimento—Death of Luigi—Thoughts of Escaping—The drying Process—Difficulty of Washing—A wounded Brigand—Assistance given by the Peasants to the Brigands—Description of the Band—A regular Feed for once in a way—Potluck—Unpleasant Sleeping Quarters—Sheepstealers.

CHAPTER VII.

May 28.—Sunday, and a lovely day; the air as clear as crystal. I counted seven separate ridges of mountains between our lair and Salerno. Each seemed to stand up clear and distinct by itself. I could distinguish the white houses of the town, and tried to fancy that I could see the Hotel Vittoria. I could distinguish two steamers, which I set down as Florio's boats, coming from or going to Palermo, and I remembered our happy voyage from that city only a little more than a fortnight ago. A trifle to the south I could distinguish the temples of Pæstum, and some ten miles to the north of these a few white houses, representing Battipaglia, where the ruffians who surrounded me had lain in waiting for so many hours. The panorama was superb. I tried to enjoy it, but my heart was too sad; I could only think of all those that were striving to procure my release.

At eleven o'clock I took out my prayer-book and went through the service, and thought of those many hundred of thousands of our Church who were then doing the same. As I read I was frequently interrupted by the brigands asking me what I was reading, and wanting to look at the book. After a few days they ceased troubling me in this manner, for they all had great respect for any prayer or other sacred book.

In the afternoon we inquired again when food was coming, but could get no other response than an angry "Who knows?" All at once whistles and other signals were heard, and immediately each grasped his gun and ran forward in a stooping position to face the danger; but the word "*Compagni*" set them all at ease again, and Lorenzo Guerino and four or five others came up. Visconti was in the greatest state of excitement, and asked if there was any more money for him.

Joy spread over his countenance as they replied in the affirmative, and seven fingers were held out to represent 7000 ducats. I wanted him to rush forward to receive his letters, but he feared the ravings with which his impatience would be met, for all letters were always read by their lordships before being handed over to us prisoners; but Don Elia's writing was too much for Manzo or Andrea, the secretary of Pepino, and Don Francesco was told to sit down by Manzo's side, and read his father's letters out loud.

More signals were now heard, the same scene of excitement was gone through, and Zacharia, a domestic of Visconti's household, was led forward, bearing bread, wine, and a little chocolate and some sweets, from Don Elia and his brother, in order, as the letter to Tomasino expressed it, " to assuage that hunger of which you complain." This of course was immediately taken by the band, and divided in equal shares, Sentouio cutting all the cheese, *supersalo*, and sausages, with scrupulous impartiality. I fortunately fell across the little basket, while Francesco Cicco had it. I saw five cakes of chocolate, and appropriated two before I could be stopped for Visconti and myself, but, alas! the women got wind of this, and came to me for some. I had to disgorge at least a third of what I had secured, and the sweets were also divided, but Visconti and I got none. They now came for my leather drinking-cup, and the enormous bottle of wine was speedily emptied, the cup being passed round full to each. The day of starvation was turned into a *festa*, but at the expense of the two Viscontis; for the supply of food, which was meant to last them till more could be sent, was eaten up at one fell swoop by these ruffians. Fifteen thousand ducats had now been paid by the family of Visconti for their two unfortunate members, and Don Elia, in his letter, pleaded great poverty, and desired to know how much more was requisite in order to free them. Many of the band demanded all the sum originally asked, viz., 40,000 ducats, equal to 6,800*l.*, but after a thoroughly Italian dispute, and many threats towards the unhappy victims, 25,000 ducats, or 4,150*l.* was the amount settled upon; and it was intimated that if this sum was not completed and sent immediately, ears and fingers would be despatched to Giffone forthwith. Poor little Tomasino was made to write in a similar strain, only that his head was to be sent, ears and all. It was a touching scene to see the poor little fellow writing his letter in a large round-hand writing.

I was now taken in hand, and told to write to the consul and my wife; but to my great grief was forbidden to write one word of English. Visconti was tutored by Manzo as to the substance of my letter, and, after a short time, two long letters were written. I was very anxious that the insurance on my life should not be forgotten to be paid. So, after a great deal of trouble, I got leave to insert the names of friends of mine in England, and with them a hint as to the insurance.

I had forgotten the date, and so mis-dated my letters the 26th instead of the 28th.*

The division of the food, eating it, and the letter-writing, had made the time pass so quickly that we had not noticed the shades of evening that had darkened around us, and down we lay again, thanking God for the merciful sending of the food, which had turned our starvation into

---

* After this I took a little piece of paper and on it endeavoured to sketch the superb view before us. All stood round me passing comments on the Inglese that was supposed to be able to do everything. (My being able to tell them the nationality of their guns and pistols had surprised them.) They did not quite like this new amusement, and in a day or two destroyed my sketch and got hold of my pencil, to the disappointment of both Visconti and myself. He was always making abstruse calculations of francs, ducats, and napoleons, and being without a pencil had always borrowed mine. This sketch was talked about to the peasants, then at Salerno, and then through the Italian journals to the English papers, magnified, of course, and many of my friends were disappointed that I have not a complete set of sketches illustrating my life among the brigands.

comparative plenty — the brigands who had brought the money having also brought a large supply of bread.

During the night there was again an alarm, but this turned out to be a false one, or rather of no account; but the next day proved it to be a spy of the troops sniffing round us. Had it been known who it was, his life would have answered for it.

May 29.—It was a cold, damp night, and in the morning, when we were awakened by the usual kick and alarm, we found everything enveloped in a dense fog; the captain told off ten men to to go with him, in order to receive the answers to our letters, and any money that might be sent.

We were sent off under the charge of Pepino, and the rest of the two bands; the Viscontis were the property of his band, while I belonged to Manzo's, unfortunately for me; for Pepino and his men had no interest in my expected ransom, and all the time I was under his charge I was miserably treated: unfair shares of food, blows, threats, and constant bullying, were what I had to put up with.

We retraced our steps of Saturday evening, and ascended the steep hill. How I groaned mentally as I dragged my legs, so stiff from the effects of the damp ground up the ascent! When we reached the top we did not descend the other side, but turned to the left and went along the narrow ridge. We experienced the same difficulties as before, on account of the sharpness of the ridge causing our passing along it to be so exceedingly dangerous. At one place an enormous precipitous rock barred the way, its flat sides overhanging on each side. After examining it all round, we found a place at one corner, where by being pulled up from above, and being pushed up from below, we succeeded one by one in ascending a few yards; and then, passing round the corner, went some way along a narrow ledge, and found at last a more practicable path; a little farther on we found two *baraque;* the boughs with which they were made looked as if they had been built only two days before, and the leaves were quite fresh, and not at all withered. "*La forza !*" was the sudden cry of all, and at once all eyes were on the ground looking for the footmarks of the soldiers, and they were immediately estimated at fifty in number.

After walking for about an hour and a half, we came to what was considered a proper place for concealing ourselves; the narrow ridge ceased suddenly, forming a precipice of some hundreds of feet, making our lair quite secure on the side facing the north, while on the west there was another precipice. On the south of the ridge and eastward there was a narrow ascent covered with brushwood and large trees; there were two enormous beech-trees in the two northern corners, and another in the south-western. We were told to lie down while Pavone and Justi cut down small trees and branches, which were placed between these trees in order to make the place more secure; in the centre there was a large stone, weighing about a ton, this was attacked next, but it was more than they could manage, as it was three parts sunk in the ground; but Sentonio and Pavone persevered, and by undermining it, and cutting a huge branch to use as a lever, it was moved out of the way to one side, and the place made level.

These operations took some time, and they were only just completed, when a sudden grasping of guns, and a movement of all in the direction from which we had come, made the hearts of us prisoners jump into our throats. I had not yet got accustomed, as I did very soon, to these sudden alarms. The brigands' senses of hearing and seeing were extraordinarily acute; their very lives depended on them; they could always detect the approach of any one many hundred yards off; I soon acquired the same habit, and often told them of the approach of those who were fetching food and water. On this occasion the blue clothing of the comer soon told them that it was one of their companions, and he rushed into the centre of the group, saying, in hurried accents, that there had been a *tradimento,* and that two companies of soldiers had surrounded the place where we had passed Saturday night and Sunday, only a few minutes after we had left it, and that we must immediately leave the neighbourhood. Many were the imprecations uttered against the troops. I cannot admit that we prisoners looked on them as likely to be our deliverers, the chances seemed one hundred to one against our being rescued by them; for the soldiers blaze away at anything moving, and the prisoners always stood the same chance of being hit as the brigands. Besides, Manzo had given strict orders to all his followers to shoot us immediately there appeared the slightest chance of our escaping; and the band

were always the most savage against me because I was an Englishman, and they feared that I would give information, when native prisoners dared not, for fear of the vengeance of the band.*
Fortunately Ferdinando brought with him a *maccatore* full of bread, which served for our breakfast; but no time was allowed us to eat it now, as all the *robe* were collected, and off we went again toward the east, walking for three or four hours down hill before we pulled up. The scenery was most monotonous, the whole way being through one interminable forest of beech trees. The path was exceedingly steep, and we often had to cling on by the branches of one tree, not leaving hold till we could stop our impetus against the stem of another.

About the middle of the day a furious thunder-

* How many are now living in terror, in consequence of having given evidence against atrocious villains, whose lives have been spared, some day perhaps to commit new atrocities! Read the history of the brothers La Gala, in Mr. Hilton's "Brigandage in Southern Italy," vol. 2.

storm came on as usual, and we all took refuge under trees from the terrific shower of rain that fell. Don Francesco and I sat crouched up under the *capote* that had been given to me. We were under a large beech, but very soon the rain came pouring down from the branches on us, but we could not move because everywhere the ground was running with water. Below us was a plain, with two villages in sight; I told Visconti that I thought it was his country, but he did not seem to know it, and laughed at me for attempting to know a place I had never seen. I told him that Giffone was a little more to our left, shut out from our sight by a mountain. (I was quite right, as it turned out; and he recalled the circumstance to my mind when I was at Giffone after my release, and he pointed out to me the mountain where we had been on that day.)

Well do I remember that day and place, for a terrible judgment fell on Luigi, one of Cerino's band. I was all the more impressed with it on account of an occurrence that took place two days before. Seeing a little cross and beads in the hands of the man, and being always on the look-out for little reminiscences, I asked him for it; but his reply was, "What! give you my life?" He explained to me, that if he lost or parted with it, he would soon lose his life. Luigi was sitting on a mass of rock a few yards from me, with Pepino, Doniella, and two or three others close to him. Between them and me on the right-hand side there was a little gap, and below the mountain was rather steep. On our left it was level for a short distance, and then rose to a great height. All at once the cry of "*La Forza*" was raised, and off they all ran, those sitting by us driving us on. Most of them ran up hill. I darted through the gap on my right, for I thought that if the troops came on when I got below I could double back towards them; but that wretch, Andrea, the executioner, come after me, and told me to stop. It was a false alarm, and Visconti and I returned back to the place we had kept dry under the beech, and sat down in our old position, but in two or three minutes some one said, "Where is Luigi?" He was not to be seen, but one of them found his *capote* where he had been sitting. Three paces from it was a precipice of about 2000 feet, and the poor fellow had in his fright gone clean over it, not having noticed the danger when he sat down. A cry of horror was raised at the discovery, and tears rose in the eyes of all his companions. I could not but feel much affected at his awful death, though at the same time I confess I counted four on my fingers, that being the number now disposed of since I had been taken by the band, and I thought to myself that the more that were killed the better chance I should have of escaping. Luigi feared the hand of man, but little thought that, by his his own act, he was rushing, with all the sins of four years' brigandage on his head, into the presence of his Maker!

The women were most affected, shedding tears; and "*povero Luigi!*" was the exclamation of all. He was a tall thin man, about forty years of age, very reserved, and with far more forethought than most Italians. He was very careful and saving; his clothing was old and full of repairs. He always mended a rent immediately. He carried on his back a wallet of sheepskin, in which were stowed away many useful articles, such as scissors, an awl for mending boots, &c., &c. His trousers fitted close to the leg, and he wore large thick woollen gaiters.

After a few minutes' lamentation they went down the mountain in order to find his body, for there was but little doubt as to his fate. After about three-quarters of an hour's descent, we were halted, while the band went a little way up the ravine on our left to search for him. They soon found him lying on the snow with which the ravine was filled. He was quite dead, with his back broken and his head smashed in. While the search for the body was going on we had been halted in the midst of some tall broom, under the charge of Pavone, and after a few minutes we went on along the narrow footpath. I was in front, and, instead of turning to the left, went straight on, Visconti, Tomasino, and Pavone following me. When the rest of the band, who had returned from their sad task, perceived us, they gave a signal cry to tell us where they were —about 300 yards on our left, on the other side of a little stream.

I now thought of attempting to escape by running along the path; but it was at least two miles to the village I had seen in the morning, and it was getting dark, and I should have had to cross two small mountains and the odds were too heavy against me; so that when Pavone found out he had mistaken the path he called out to me, and I turned back with the rest. He was in an awful rage, danced in the air with passion, and cocked his gun ready for use, had any one of us attempted to escape. Had the path been well defined and level, and the time earlier in the day, I think I should have attempted it, for I was at least fifty yards a-head, and before he could have fired at me I should have been a hundred yards off; and I know that he had only a musket, and before he could have loaded again I should have been at a safe distance; but the two miles to the town and the difficulties of the way determined me to wait for a more favourable opportunity. I was always on the look-out to escape, and constantly bore in mind which direction would take me to the town; but Pavone and Scope never let me go out of their sight, and I could never move my position, either day or night, without the exclamation "*Che fate?*" or "*Dove andate?*" I could not even sit up without being told to lie down directly. (I never had but one chance, which I will relate hereafter.) When we joined the rest of the band, I found them all plunged in grief;

they had stripped poor Luigi of all that might prove useful, but his clothes, being old and ragged, were left upon him.

Poor fellow! He was left on the snow, just as he lay when they found him; and in a few days the vultures that abound in this district, would no doubt leave nothing but his bones to bleach in the mountain air, probably never again to be seen by human eye. I asked for some little memento of him, and they gave me the little bag full of pictures of saints, which Italians of the lower class always carry on their persons. In it were also three little leaves and some pieces of the gum used for incense in the churches.

After a short time, on we went; it was now dark, and we left the path, and directed our course through a thick wood along the bottom of the mountain. The trees were very wet, and as we pushed the branches on one side in order to pass, we were soaked through by the falling drops; our feet, too, and trousers, were thoroughly drenched, and

I groaned inwardly at the prospect of our night's rest, or rather the want of it.

After two hours' more walking, when we were nearly dead beat, a low whisper of *"fuoco,"* was raised by those ahead, and we were told to walk *" cete a cete"*—that is, as silently as possible; and in five minutes we were halted, while two went on to see the cause of the fire in the wood, as the soldiers were known to be all round, and it was feared that this might be one of their encampments. It proved, however, to be only the fire of some woodcutters, so we were moved on at a signal from the advanced guard, and in three minutes we were warming ourselves round the welcome blaze. Two peasants were there when we came up, but in a few minutes, two more, who had retired on our approach, advanced from the darkness round. These were old friends, if one could judge from the kisses and warm embraces with which they were greeted by several of the band. To our great delight, on one side of the fire a tall rock overhung a little, and had thus kept the ground under it quite dry; this was strewed with dry moss, and Visconti and I sat down on it, and to our joy were allowed to remain there. I was dreadfully hungry, not having had anything to eat since our meagre breakfast of literally only a mouthful of black bread. My eye fell on a *maccatore*, hung on a corner of the rock, in which was a little Indian-corn bread. I asked one of the wood-cutters if he would give it me; but with curses from the band, I was told not to touch it. It was handed over to one of them, and two more loaves being produced, the whole was divided in equal shares, and I ate my portion with gratitude, thanking God for the unexpected fire and shelter that we had fallen in with.

I took off my boots and socks, and dried them as well as I could, but before they were half dry I was made to put them on for fear of our being surprised, and my not being able to run away barefooted.

This fear caused them always to forbid my removing any of my clothing for washing purposes. I stood up and dried my capote and garments as long as I was allowed to do so, turning round and round, as though roasting on a jack. It was near midnight before we laid down, curled up on the moss that was to have served as the wood-cutters' couch. They sat round the fire, conversing with the band, who thus heard all the news of the district, and were told of all the movements of the troops. Visconti and I slept soundly, but were woke up as usual at an hour before daybreak.

May 30.—We left the wood-cutters, who were presented with a napoleon as a *complimento,* and we ascended higher up the mountain. An hour's walk brought us to a level space, concealed by trees all round. On one side a gully, where the winter rains ran down, formed a straight path down the mountain side. We had to lie down on the wet grass, but soon forgot these little cares in more sleep. When we awoke again, at about seven or eight o'clock, we asked for bread, but were told that we should have none all day, and that there would be no water.

In the middle of the day there was one of the usual alarms, which proved to be caused by four or five more of the band who had come to join us. With them was one of the women—Concetta. Poor girl! she had been shot right through the upper part of the arm through the accidental discharge of one of the guns. The ball had broken the bone in two, and the arm was suspended and wrapped up in numerous pocket-handkerchiefs. She did not utter a groan or murmur. Much concern for her was exhibited by all, and all strove to do what little they could for her. Natural ammoniated water was used to bathe and dress it with, and a shirt was torn up and unravelled to furnish lint. Cicco acted as surgeon, and no one could have been more tender in his treatment of her. No food was given to us all day, but to my joy I found in my pocket a morsel of bread that I had forgotten. I shared it with Don Francesco, and then turned out my pockets, and picking out the dirt, ate the crumbs which I found there. We heard from the newly arrived brigands to-day that the troops were all round us. Great caution was observed. In the evening two or three ascended the mountain to search for snow, and in about an hour and a half returned with a great mass carried on a *stick*. We ate a quantity of this to assuage our thirst, not having had any water for twenty-four hours. I found this want of drink very trying at first, but soon had to get accustomed to it, and to fare still worse.

The news was also spread round to-day that the Government was going to pay for me; and that, as this was so, they were going to demand a much larger ransom. This disturbed me dreadfully, and kept me awake all night. I talked much to Visconti on the subject. He told me that it was very bad news for me, and might be the cause of my being detained a long time. Tomasino, like a boy as he was, took the greatest pleasure in worrying me, declaring to me that the brigands had told him again that if the Government paid they would require 1,000,000 ducats; and that, even if I paid this, I should have plenty left, because of the great riches which they all declared I possessed. He also greatly annoyed his cousin, who declared that he was a *vera musca*, alias *musquito*. He certainly was most tiresome, and I am afraid that at times I quite lost my patience with him, and frequently kept my stick by my side as a reminder for him not to come too near me. To add to our misery, in the evening we had more rain. It seemed of little use drying our clothes, or spreading them on a branch in the sun, for they were no sooner dry than wet again, and when once soaked, the *capote* took two or three days to get moderately dry—perfectly so it never was at this period. To-night I discovered that the muslin turban, that I used to wear on my straw-hat, when rolled up and doubled, made a capital comforter to wear round my neck at night. I never omitted to use this afterwards, until the weather got too warm, when it made a secure shelter for those disgusting little animals from which I suffered so much a little later.

Had all the sufferings I had to endure eventually come upon me during the first days, I do not know how I should have borne them; but they seemed to come on gradually, and what I thought dreadful at first, I got to think little of afterwards.

May 31.—It rained nearly all night, and there was a cold, cutting wind, so we accordingly woke up in the morning, if possible, colder and stiffer than usual, and we had to straighten our

knees entirely by rubbing them, as no fire could
be made on account of the troops around us. We
were not allowed to move or speak all the first
part of the day, fifty soldiers having passed along
the valley a little after the break of day, and there
were two posts not far from us. The wood-
cutters, who had been busy felling trees all yesterday, and the sound of whose strokes had
enlivened the solitude, were quite silent to-
day. I presume they had left the neighbourhood,
evidently fearing being implicated with the doings
of the band, should the troops discover where we
were; for the peasants were thrown into prison
on the slightest suspicion of providing the band
with food; and very properly so, too, for without
the aid of the peasantry it would be impossible
for brigandage to exist. As it is, the peasants
cannot resist the high price paid for everything
by the brigands, and when they meet, like all the
Italians of this class, they cannot refrain from
gossiping about everything that goes on in the

district, particularly the movements of the troops, and the constant *complimentos* paid to them make them anxious to impart everything that is of importance to these outlaws. Suddenly, about the middle of the day, soldiers were seen on the top of the mountain opposite to us, through the telescopes which were in constant use. This created great excitement, and we were made to lie flat on the ground, and not allowed to move, while one or two of the men ascended the highest trees near, and, with the glasses, reported every movement. The soldiers, about fifty in number, lay down on the ground and rested for half an hour, and then disappeared over the top of the mountain; we saw nothing more of them, but the band was uneasy all day, some one constantly ascending the trees in order to keep a good lookout. They astonished me with the ease and rapidity with which they climbed, taking hold of a branch and swinging themselves up in an instant. As soon as it was considered safe we went

ITALIAN BRIGANDS. 241

farther up the mountain, to my great annoyance; for, instead of the places that we had kept dry, we had to lie down just where we were told, for we were never allowed to use our own discretion, but were frequently made to settle down in a nest of nettles, thorns, or thistles. When we got here a little bread was produced, but so little that it only served to make us more hungry than before. With the bread came the news that Victor Emmanuel was going to pay my ransom himself. This was bad news for me, for, as long as there was a chance of it being true, they would keep asking the 50,000 ducats.

I amused myself this afternoon in learning all I could about brigandage in the province of Salerno, by asking all at various times. I concluded that there were in all about seventy brigands under four captains, and this turned out to be very near the mark: Giardullo and his band consisting of about thirty, and the two bands with which I was connected, being in number forty-two. Of these seven were runaway soldiers, viz., Manzo, Ferdinando, Guange, Amendolo,* Carini, and two others; Giuseppe, from what I could hear, came from Naples. Cicco had once some little amount of money, on which he lived before being a brigand; Andrea, the executioner, had, by his own account, been a master farrier, according to others, a master shoemaker; the others all had been agricultural labourers or shepherds, excepting my friend Lorenzo Guerino, who had been a sawyer and carpenter. Nearly all had committed homicide. Manzo, however, and Guange, by the account of all, were free from this crime; the former on one occasion shot a follower for refusing to obey his orders, and they all said he would do it again in a moment, if necessary; but from my experience, a stick laid over their shoulders was the punishment when they would not be silent when told. Guange had not disliked his life as soldier, and said that the allow-

* In the Appendix will be found an account of this worthy.

ance of food was good, but he had been absent one day without leave, and fearing the consequences, took to the woods.

Three or four of the band had joined only a few days before my capture; these had their *carte di soggiorno* with them, and often looked at them and showed them to me. They were still dressed in their peasant dresses, and it was long ere they were able to obtain their brigand clothing; but before I left them, they all had gradually picked up the proper uniform. This they obtained from the peasants when getting food, and paid for out of their own share of my ransom.

Malone Zaza, a native of Acerno, who was one of these recruits, was only eighteen years old, and used to take the milk round to the houses in the town; but one day a friend tried to cheat him out of five ducats, equal to sixteen shillings and eightpence; this so enraged him that a fatal blow from his knife compelled him to become a brigand. He was not *in giro*, as they call it, when I was taken, and thus he had no share in the money; for those only who are present at the capture divide the spoil. All share equally, the captain having no more than the others, and a certain amount being kept back for general expenses.

At about five o'clock, the tinkling of the bells below told us that a flock of sheep was passing from one pasture to another. Pepino, who was very impatient under a lack of food, jumped up, and with Generoso and Andrea started off to see what they could procure. In about an hour they returned leading a fine fat sheep and a goat, which were soon killed, and in less than an hour there was nothing left but the head and bones. Excepting the paunch, every morsel was eaten. When we had got meat, there was a difficulty in cooking it, on account of our position.

With the troops in the neighbourhood a fire was most dangerous, and many of the men declared it was madness to think of lighting it. But we had had too little the last three days to think of foregoing our promised repast, so two of the old hands cut out an oblong hole in a sloping place, and then another at right angles at the end of it; the fire was made with the greatest caution in this, and the pot put over it; two *capotes* were placed in front, so as to conceal any gleam of light; every piece of wood was dried before it was put on and the fire very slowly fed, and by these means all smoke was avoided; they certainly did make the most smokeless fires I ever saw. When the internal *bonne-bouche* was pronounced ready, we were invited to dip with them into the pot. I took out my pocket-fork and avoided scalding my fingers, theirs were like horn, and no heat ever seemed to hurt them. This fork was much admired, and when I was told that I had eaten my share, which was always on these occasions about a quarter of what each of them ate, one of them took it from me and used it himself, but returned it when the course was finished. The meat was all divided into shares, and, to Visconti's horror, he had to eat it without bread. For drink we had to eat snow, all the water being drunk by our captors, who refused to give us any.

To-night the place where I was told to sleep was the next but one to poor Concetta, whose arm was getting worse every hour, and now began to emit a most nauseous odour. The wind, unfortunately, blew towards me, and, as I was only about four feet from her, my feelings can easily be described. The flesh round the wound had turned quite yellow, and each time it was dressed a quantity of thick matter was removed; this, with the dirty lint, was merely thrown a yard or two off, and there being a plague of flies which immediately covered any animal matter, this made me most nervous, lest they should bite me, and thus communicate the poison to my system. How they worried me, perpetually settling on me! All the care in the world would not keep them off; they always disappeared as it grew dark, but then the mosquitos came out, and their demoniacal drumming nearly drove me distracted; but I soon found out that our simple food prevented that inflammation and pain that their bites occasion in civilised life. Two or three hours after dark Ferdinando, with three others, returned with one live sheep and one that they had already killed and skinned.

CHAPTER VIII.

THE CAPTIVE'S DIARY CONTINUED: JUNE 1 TO 7.

Wood-carving—The Wounded Girl—A Tantalizing View—Victims—The Captives not introduced—A Thunderbolt—Rain, Rain—Three under a Cloak—Ill Treatment from Cerino's Band—Their abject fear of Death—A Blow from Cerino — Consolation—New Arrivals — Screwing up—A Scrimmage with Generoso— The greedy Cerino—An Instalment of my Ransom Arrives —The Proposal to the Brigands to leave the Country in an English Ship—The Lesson of the "Aunis"—What became of the 10,000 francs—Gambling—Visconti is appointed my Agent—Pleasant Position of his Family—I am the only Captive—Quarrels—The *Argumentum Baculinum*—I am invited to Gamble.

CHAPTER VIII.

June 1.—We spent "the glorious 1st of June" in the same place. How long the day seemed, with nothing to do but to brood over my griefs! For want of anything better to do, I began whittling the stem of a wild jasmine with my penknife, and amused myself in cutting out a little cross, which I meant to send to my wife at the first opportunity. Much interest was taken by the brigands in seeing me cut what all Roman Catholics, however humble and degraded in position, revere so much ; *è molto talento,* was the constant remark when they saw me at work with the minute blade, the temper of which astonished them so much. We had no bread either to-day or the next day ; but they gorged themselves with meat. I preserved as much as

I could save in my pocket, not knowing when we should get more; two or three sausages had been kept back from the last division for Concetta, whose arm was getting worse and worse. Poor girl! she did not utter a sound of complaint, but merely clenched her teeth together and hissed through them when they were dressing her wound and cutting off the dead flesh with a pair of scissors. I translated a few verses of the Psalms to her, and entreated her to think over her past life and ask forgiveness.

She seemed to attend with great earnestness to what I said, and when I had finished she entreated me to pray for her, and was not satisfied till I had promised to do so. I told her that, unless she could get medical aid, it was impossible to hope for any improvement, and that she must prepare for the worst.

Early in the afternoon I was delighted at seeing all the band rise up from the ground, and sling their guns on their shoulders. This was the certain

sign of a move. We were soon told to get up.
I tied up my *capote* with a little piece of string
and a cotton handkerchief that Manzo had given
me, and with these managed to sling it on my
back; it was rather heavy, and I had found great
difficulty in carrying it on my left arm, for I
wanted both hands—one to carry my invaluable
stick, and with the other I grasped the low
branches of the trees in ascending and descend-
ing the steep places.

My heart quite bled when I saw that poor
dying Concetta walking along in the rear, supported between two men. We were between
two or three hours in reaching the top, passing
many frightful ravines—some of them, which
we had to cross, full of snow; this was not
like the freshly-fallen snow, but, being constantly penetrated by the moisture from the
thawed surface, had crystallized into grains about
the size of hempseed, and these were all frozen
together, so that some trouble and force were

necessary in cutting out a lump to eat. At one of these places we stopped to rest for some time, while Concetta, and those with her, were toiling up the steep ascent to join us. When they came up the poor girl could hardly stand, and threw herself down on the ground, and asked me if I had any bread, for I always kept, if possible, a tiny piece, and invariably ate a little mouthful after our nauseous meat diet. I had a piece the size of a walnut in my pocket, which I could not refuse her; and it was quite a pleasure to see the expression on her face as I handed it to her, and I felt well rewarded for my self-denial.

The usual precautions were taken at the top, and on all being pronounced safe, we rested again for the stragglers to come up. Here there was another false alarm; they all ran, but I never moved, hoping that if the soldiers appeared, I should have a chance of escape. I took out my little book and began to read, to the great disgust of several of them, who disliked nothing more than seeing me perfectly indifferent when they all were showing fear.

From this elevated point I again saw the mountains with their jagged peaks close to Salerno, the point stretching out to Amalfi, and the blue Mediterranean. How I longed to be on it, in one of those tiny fishing-boats with lateen sails, that were speeding their way to Salerno!

As we walked along the top, I was constantly asked *Che vedete?* for the idea that I was enjoying the magnificent view was the last thing that entered their heads. We soon came up to a place where a dreadfully steep bank between two high precipices led far away down the mountain, reaching very nearly to the bottom. The greatest care had to be taken, for if I had once slipped it would have been impossible to have stopped rolling down some thousands of feet. There was a rank vegetation which concealed the loose stones, which were in great abundance, and this made our descent very difficult. Often these would be set in motion, to the great danger of those below, who had to jump quickly out of the way to avoid them. I think this, more than anything else, raised the ire and curses of the band, for a stone, once set rolling, generally with a great noise keeps rolling down to the bottom, giving notice to anyone below that somebody is above, which might be the means of giving the troops warning of the proximity of the band. As we descended we saw several fires, which marked the spot where the shepherds were stationed for the night, and where they make the cheese and *racotta* from the milk yielded by the flocks of sheep grazing on these southern slopes of the mountains.

We no sooner began to descend than we left behind us the dense forests on the northern side. When we came to the level of the first fire, two of the band went towards it, and soon returned with one of the shepherds, who carried a barrel of water, which shepherds always have with them. This was a great luxury, for I had only eaten snow for the last few days. I got up and stepped forward to it, but was instantly told in a brutal way to go back again; for a captive is never allowed to see or speak to a peasant. They do this (as I said before) on account of the peasant, who fears being recognised and denounced afterwards when the ransom is paid. In a short time the barrel was passed to me. I took it by each end, and drank, after their fashion, out of the bung-hole in the centre. A little Indian-corn bread was also divided between us, and Visconti and I enjoyed the remains of our cold goat, which we had tied up together in my pocket-handkerchief, having nothing else to carry it in.

When we approached to the next fire the same precautionary measures were repeated; but as it was in our route, we waited till the usual signal (a lighted brand waved in the air) was made by those who had been sent on in advance. The shepherds always tried to put out their fires on the approach of the brigands. I suppose this was for their own protection, lest anyone should see that visitors were with them. More bread was obtained, and a little new cheese. The next fire was treated in the same way, but we were never allowed to join the circle collected round for the usual ten minutes' gossip, to hear the news. Immediately after leaving the last fire, we crossed a stream and proceeded along a good path on the other side. Visconti was disappointed in not seeing his shepherd, who he thought was in this neighbourhood. After about an hour we left this path and made our way through the brushwood. We soon came to a range of cliffs, on the face of which were many caverns. At last we came to one with a dry stony bottom, about fifteen feet high. We were told to lie down, and with guards on each side of us, we were allowed to sleep. We were roused by the kicks of our guardians, and we awoke with severe pain in all our limbs, from sleeping in the bitter cold. There was not sufficient cover in front of the cave to make it safe during the daytime.

June 2.—It had rained in the night, and we had, therefore, the satisfaction of getting wet in proceeding to a place under the rocks, with plenty of brushwood before it, where we were to stop all day. We had to ask several times before we got a portion of the bread procured from the shepherds. Pepino and his consort Doniella kept nearly all for themselves, and would hardly give us any. The rest of the band had plenty in their pockets, which they had secured when at the fires of the shepherds. This evening we went to a large roomy cavern that had evidently been made use of by the flocks of sheep, for the ground was covered with abundant signs of their recent presence. Visconti and I picked out the cleanest and driest place we could find in one corner, but we were made to get up and lie down in a very dirty and wet place, with water dripping on us from above. Andrea, the executioner, and two women guarded us, while the others went off foraging. I sat up for a minute, but our wary guard made me lie down again, fearing a sudden rush on him. On these occasions our guards always stood up at a little distance, and never took their eyes off us. In the night the band came back with some water, but nothing else; we were in the same part for the next three days, moving our sleeping-place each night.

One night we were asked if we liked milk, and were told that we were to have some. It took us half an hour to walk to the appointed place, where we found a great wooden milk-pail, about two feet high, half full. Some was poured out into a smaller pail, and some bread sopped in it. We were then told to fall to. This was the first time that I had used my wooden spoon, that I had spent so many hours in cutting from the root of the beech-tree; it served capitally for eating the bread, but it could not compete with the enormous deep spoons used in these districts for skimming the *racotta* off the remains of the milk. One was lent to me, but I preferred taking up the great pail and having a good draught out of it. I never lost an opportunity of telling them that milk was very good for an Englishman, and I always found that they gave me more than my share of it, whenever we were so lucky as to obtain any. Some *racotta* was also broken up in some milk, and this made it taste just like cream. The pails were left to be fetched away by the shepherds. Well do I remember that spot, for the rising ground on three sides brought to my mind some of the theatres cut out of the hill sides in Greece. The bottom was level, and then the ground sloped away to the river far below. Our halting-place was covered with a low broom in full blossom. The moon was shining brightly on all the surrounding mountains; not a breath of air was stirring, and the only sound to be heard was that of the distant torrent below.

June 6.—The night was passed in the caves as before, and before daybreak we went back towards the place where we had found the milk, and spent the day on the hill side. We were forbidden to speak or move the whole day. The bright sky of last night had left us, and all above us was covered with the blackest clouds, when suddenly, about midday, the storm broke in a thunderbolt, which passed whizzingly close over our heads, apparently only a few feet from us, and went right down and seemed to strike the ground near the stream below us. I never in my life heard anything to equal the awful crackling and roaring sound of its passage. We were all amazed, and one of the brigands said " it seeks the water." They all crossed themselves, and several hurried off to seek the shelter of the grottos. I wished to do the same, but was not allowed to move. I had no sooner put on my *capote*, than a perfect sheet of water fell on us. I took Visconti under the cloak with me; when Lorenzo, who had always treated me well, came close up and made me give him part too. I was in the centre; we put our covering over our heads, drew up our knees to our noses, and there we sat five mortal hours growling at everything! Poor Visconti was in the most fearful state of despair, although two men, who had joined us in the morning, had brought the joyful news to him that the 10,000 ducats that remained to complete his ransom had been paid. How I envied him! He did not seem to feel sure of his liberty, and told me that he should not feel safe till he had arrived in his own house. How miserable I felt—no letters, no money!

Three weeks had now elapsed since my capture, and during the last week especially I had been badly treated. Pepino's band, who were to have no share in my expected ransom, looked on me as a nuisance, and grudged every morsel of food they gave me. Except during the two days when we had meat, I do not think I had, in all, more than was really enough for one day's consumption. They always made a point of speaking to me in a most brutal manner, without an atom of kindness, and they constantly threatened my life with their guns, revolvers, and knives. One great game was thrusting their knives quickly between my body and arms. I never allowed myself to show the slightest fear, and always told them that it was nothing to die, it was soon over, and that the next world was far better.

They all have the most abject fear of death, and I always tried to impress them with the idea that Englishmen never fear to die; and that if they wished it, they were perfectly welcome to take my life, as it would save me and my friends so much trouble. I felt sure that in a short time they would discontinue trying to frighten me when they found out that I only laughed at their attempts, and ridiculed them for their fear of death.

But I am forgetting the storm of rain. The cloak, though a good cover for two during an ordinary shower, was not of much use for three with the flood that was pouring down. The water collected when the cloak was stretched between our heads, and then dripped, or rather ran, through in streams, each one pulling it more over himself, and accordingly drenching his neighbour. When I attempted a change, I always said, "*E melior cosi*," but the reply came, "*E melior per voi, ma peggior per me.*" I, being in the centre, came off best, but the best was bad enough. The water also collected in pools under us, and at last ran in a perfect stream. At five o'clock we were soaked through, and so cramped from our position that we could not move. I looked forward to a fearful night, and was as miserable as I could possibly be, and very hungry, for we had had nothing to eat or drink all day.

When the word came to us to get ready to start off to join the rest of the band, I asked how many hours walking, and eight fingers held up told me what I had to expect. Before we started I asked Pepino whether any money or letters had come for me. I was standing on the edge of a mound, and was unprepared for the blow which I received for an answer. I lost my balance and fell down, hurting myself badly on the inside of my leg from striking it against a large stone. What a rage I felt in! I could have knocked him over on the spot with pleasure, but was obliged to choke it down as best I could. I asked him what harm I had done, and was told to be quiet and not to speak a word. They were very savage that no money had come for me at the same time that it had come for the Viscontis; and Andrea reproached me with having caused the death of four of the band who had died *for love of me!* Justi came up to me and said, "*Povero Cristiano,*" and told me that Pepino was a brute and that I was not to care for what he said or did.

We now began to descend towards the river, passing along and over the terraces of earth in which the Italians always cultivate the mountain sides; the ground was sopping from the heavy rain, and therefore very slippery. I more than once fell, on one occasion making a bad wound on my shin, the scar of which I still retain. It was very difficult to pass the torrent, which was three times the size it was when we had crossed a few days before.

They told me to drink if I required it, for we should not pass more water. I used the leather cup which Mr. Aynsley had given me in parting, and which I always lent to Visconti. The favourite way with the brigands was to lie down at full length and lap up the water like dogs. Some of them would pick the leaves of a plant that always seemed to grow near water, and, doubling them up in their left hands, formed extempore drinking-cups. We soon found the mule-track, or *scorza* as they call it, and, turning towards the north, walked along in Indian file, at the rate of about three and a half miles an hour. After half an hour we were halted while some of the band went to get some milk, and we waited for an hour before they returned empty-handed. During this hour I got permission to walk up and down a little, for it was bitterly cold, and I was wet through and afraid to sit down. While doing this I heard some signals in a low voice from the mountain opposite and reported them. They were at once answered, and down came six or eight men, who had been sent by Manzo to look for us. They were all wet through and half starved, not having been able to get any bread. They were desperate when they found that we had none to give them, and all drew their belts and bands round their waists an inch tighter. They said that they had taken us for *bersaglieri* from my walking up and down like a sentry.

Soon it began to rain so hard that even these ruffians grumbled, and, turning up a little path to the left, went to a large dry cave. I fortunately found a place that must have served as a bed to some one; it was made of the dry leaves that wrap round the spikes of Indian corn, and it was so soft after the hard ground I had been used to, that I had no sooner lain down than I dropped off into a sound sleep, though my clothes were wet through. It seemed hardly a minute before I was kicked up and told to take my place in the line. It had left off raining, but it was very dark, and we had to feel our way up the mountain side. With the intervals of two or three short rests, we kept on walking for four or five hours up the pass, till, at last, the great caution which was used, and the freshness of the wind, told me that we were close to the top. After waiting a short time, while scouts were sent out, they began to break out swearing at the rest of the band not being where they expected to find them, and, being very tired, they were more brutal than usual. We were always made to lie down immediately a halt was called, for fear we might give them the slip.

The wolf cry was now made, but there was no response. Again and again was the cry of *wow-wow, wow-wow,* uttered in their peculiar way, but it was useless; when one proposed that they should go farther on to the left, where the mountain rose higher, and, after a quarter of an hour's more walking, the signal-calls were again made, and this time with more success; for in the distance a faint answer was heard, and we went on towards the place where the bark came from. The ascent was exceedingly steep, and Generoso, who was behind me, kept hitting and poking me with the barrel of his gun, because I did not ascend as quickly as he wished, though I was close behind the man before me. At last, I turned round in a pretended rage, and with my stick in both hands raised it over his head. He shrank back and brought his gun up to his shoulder with an oath. Two or three ran up. I caught hold of him, but at the same time they abused me, and seemed taken quite aback at the idea of a *ricattato* threatening one of themselves. I told them that I walked as well as they did, and I would not be bullied, so it was no use attempting it—that they might kill me if they wished, and the sooner the better.

I found this answer capitally, and I was never touched again while on the march, and it was from this moment that they began to respect me a little for my apparent disregard of death; and when we arrived at the camp fire it was immediately narrated how I had threatened to kill a *companion*—this being the term they always use when speaking of one another. How joyful I felt when I saw the cheerful gleam of the enormous wood fire! Manzo and the rest of the band were round it, making in all forty-three in number. When we entered the circle they all seemed very glad to see me, for they had had no news of me since the Sunday, when the soldiers were disappointed in surrounding us, and they had feared that some harm might have befallen our division of the band. They gave me a large piece of bread and a lump of wet raw bacon, and I went to the fire, and pushing in through those round it, began to toast the bacon.

Pepino, who, being very tired, had lagged behind, now came up, but too late for any of the bread, which had all been given away. He saw me with my nice large piece, and suddenly snatched it out of my hands. I immediately complained to Manzo, and told him that his lieutenant was no better than a petty thief to rob me of a piece of bread, and I began to rave against all of them; for we had had no food for twenty-four hours, and after our long walk I was very hungry, and had only just congratulated myself on the piece of bread that had been given me—very different in size to anything I had been used to when under the charge of Pepino Cerino; but to my joy, one of the band took compassion on me and gave me his own piece, which I accepted with thanks. In a short time all but the sentinels threw themselves down on the wet ground, and were fast asleep; but I kept near the glowing embers of the fire and dried myself as much as I could, and sat up on a little piece of stone, for I was still damp, and my *capote* was wringing wet, and there was a bitterly cold wind blowing, and I thought it was better to forego a little sleep than catch a cold, which means a fever in these woods.

June 7.—In two hours, I saw the eastern sky light up, and gradually it grew quite light; we were now removed two or three hundred yards off to a small open part, surrounded by very large beech-trees. There was a large rock covered on one side with moss, standing up in the centre, and I sat under this to be out of the wind, and basked in the sun, which was now rising higher and higher.

Presently Visconti came to me and told me that a guide had come with money and letters for me: one from Mr. Aynsley and one from the consul, but none from my dear wife. How anxious I was for her! In neither letter was there a line about her health, and her name was only once mentioned. No message to me and nothing to console me; the letter from Mr. Aynsley was in English, but merely details of what had been done. The letter from the consul was in Italian, and meant for the band to read; and its tone gave them confidence in him, and they always expressed a high opinion of their trust in his word and actions.

They asked me if my companion, whom they had let go, was to be trusted, and if he would be faithful to me. I told them that he was an Englishman, and all Englishmen could trust in each other; and that I felt sure that he was doing and would do all possible for me, for I was hostage for him, and suffering for him as well as for myself. Manzo now came up and told me that 500 *marengi* had arrived for me, and he wanted to know what my friends meant by sending such a sum, and said that, if they did not send a large sum at once, he would send them my head. He was in a great rage, and I told him he had better do so at once, as it would save trouble, for it was impossible for my wife to get much money in Italy, as we were foreigners. He gave me a letter from the consul to him, entreating both him and the band to leave the country in an English ship of war. This, however, they were not inclined to do, for they all feared that they would be thrown into the sea immediately they were on board; and they mentioned the case of the four brigands (meaning Papa, d'Avanzo, and the brothers La Gala) who, as they said, tried to leave Italy in a French*

* For a full account of the escape of these villains from the

ship, after security had been promised them, and had then been betrayed. They also said that the soldiers would shoot them on their way to the sea. It appeared that the consul's letter, which had been dictated by the prefect of Salerno, and which informed the brigands of the consent of the Government having been given to the plan, was delivered to Manzo's brother, but he, although bearing a pass from General Balegno, and carrying letters sealed with H. B. M.'s consular seal, was arrested by a subordinate officer in command of a detachment, and nothing was heard of him for nearly a week. When the matter came to Mr. Bonham's ears, he immediately procured the messenger's release, and another letter was forwarded to the band containing the same proposal. It was now, how-

---

fate they so well deserved, see Count Maffei's book, and also Mr. Hilton's, vol. 2. The case of the passengers of the "Aunis" is notorious all over Italy as a signal failure of justice.

ever, too late, as the brigands had heard how the soldiers had respected the first messenger.

I suggested that three or four should go first to see if it were safe, but I was not able to do anything with them. The man who had brought up my money and letters now appeared, and Visconti was very excited, for he thought that this would be the guide to take him home to Giffone, as the news of all his money having been paid proved to be correct, and he was told that both he and his little cousin Tomasino were to be set at liberty during the day. They were in the highest state of glee at the hopes of seeing their friends again. Don Francesco told me all about his wife and two little children. He had not had a line from her all the time he had been in the mountains, but had only heard of her through his father's letters.

How wretched all this made me feel! I thought of all those dear to me, and wondered when I should see them again, the horrible fear being over me of the brigands keeping me, while they tried to extort a large sum from the Italian Government; for they all told me that, if the country paid for me, they would require a far larger sum than 50,000 ducats.

I now saw the captain sit down and spread out a *capote*, and on this he counted out the 10,000 francs sent up for me. The money was all in half napoleons, and was sent in this form because my friends thought that it would go farther than if sent in whole napoleons. Fifteen napoleons were then handed to each of the thirty men that had aided in the capture, and the balance of fifty napoleons were kept back by Manzo for general expenses.

No sooner was the money divided, than little groups were formed for the purpose of gambling, a similar operation having just taken place with the 10,000 ducats (equal to 1700*l.*) paid by Visconti. The captain very soon lost his money, and two or three hundred napoleons more; so he left off playing, and in a sulky humour came up to me, and made me write a number of letters. Visconti was told to help me, and I was told to write them all in Italian, and not to put one word in English. I wrote one to the consul, one to Mr. Aynsley, and one to my wife, entreating her to write and tell me how she was. I was also made to write one to the prefect of Salerno, requesting him to withdraw the forces, and not to take any steps that would injure the band, for that any injury to them would be retaliated on me, and that it was the prefect's fault I was taken, for he had left the road unguarded on the afternoon of the 15th of May, and that he would have to answer for it. When the letters were finished, Manzo read them carefully over, and made me add the postscripts, one of which was to the effect that the 10,000 francs just sent were not enough to keep me in bread.

The man who had brought up my money

and letters (and who was not one of Visconti's servants), had also brought a quantity of jewellery for Pepino's band, consisting of watches, gold chains, and rings; these were all brought for my inspection, and I was asked to value them, which I did to the satisfaction of the brigands. One chain I told them was too light, and was not good gold; this was given back to the guide, who was told that, if he tried to cheat them, they would kill him. He declared that it was good gold, but they would have nothing to do with it.

Visconti and I now had a long talk together; he told me that he would do all he could for me, that Manzo had ordered him to receive my letters and send them to and fro, and that he was to find guides in order to transmit my money to the band; and that, if his father did not do so in a satisfactory manner, his family would be all killed, his house burnt down, all the olive and chestnut-trees belonging to the family destroyed and the sheep and cattle slaughtered.* He entreated me to keep up my spirits, but not to expect to get away without paying a large sum of money, for they had good information that I was very rich, and could pay the amount demanded easily. I requested him to go as soon as he could to Naples, in order to see my wife, and tell her that I was quite well, and that it was necessary to send money, and to advise my friends what was best to be done under the circumstances. I also gave him the little cross I had cut to take to her, and a list of warm clothing and other little things that I required. He would not take anything written in English, or even a private note, because he said the captain would kill him if he found it out.

All at once he gave a little scream of joy at the sight of his old family servant, Fortunato Tedesco, who had come up to act as guide to take him to Giffone. The old shepherd looked delighted to see

* See Appendix.

his masters, kissed them both, and took off his hat to me. He brought up some food for them, and some cherries, but this was all taken at once by the band and divided into equal shares. How I enjoyed the cherries! I had had no vegetable food for so long, that nature seemed to rejoice at such a change of diet.

Three or four men now appeared, each with a sack of bread on his shoulders, and a quantity of cheese. This was hailed with joy, and a present of half a napoleon given to each man. It was about five o'clock when Visconti was told to get ready to go. He kissed me in the Italian fashion, and then kissed the band all round; two of them gave Tomasino little rings as keepsakes, for he was a great favourite with all of them, and Manzo gave them a napoleon between them; and taking Don Francesco on one side, cautioned him about revealing anything concerning the band; for, if he did so, they would come and kill him. Tomasino was told to say that the band was only twelve in number, and not to talk about them much. Fortunato gave Visconti his shepherd's crook as a walking-stick, and in a few minutes they were out of sight.

I then gave myself up to grief, I felt so desolate and miserable at the sight of their going away free, and leaving me behind alone, that I could not control myself; I threw myself on the ground in despair. Justi and Lorenzo came up to me and tried to console me, telling me to cheer up, for when my money was paid, I should be free too. I thought it better to put a good face on it, and so got up and walked about two hundred yards to where the sentinels were placed. I found we were on a platform about ten yards wide and two hundred yards long. On three sides the ground sloped down steeply, so that they could run down hill on three sides, while the soldiers would have to ascend the other side, they could run into the dense forest, and soon would have been lost to sight. This was the favourite form of lair with the brigands, and they generally halted when they found a spot like this. From the end where the sentinels were, there was a splendid view right over the plain of Salerno.

It was beautifully clear, and I could see far out to sea. I was only allowed to be here two or three minutes, and I was told to go back to where I had been all the morning. I tried to persuade them to let me remain, but with no avail. As I went back, I passed where all the women were sitting: they were hard at work hemming silk and cotton pocket-handkerchiefs; they had different coloured silks to hem, with scissors, thimbles, and all that was requisite. I noticed that their needles were much shorter than those of English make. The gambling was still going on, and many were the furious quarrels that this gave rise to; the captain had to interfere constantly, and would often have to belabour two or three with a stick before he could reduce them to silence. They wanted me to play with them, but I was not sure whether they would pay their losses; so I tried them first with *confetti*, letting two or three be seen, and then clenching my fist. They guessed four, but I had over fifty in my hand. They laughed when I asked them to pay, so I took the hint, and declined all gambling with them.

A loaf of bread was now given to each, and preparations made for departure. I learnt that Manzo and about twenty-five men were going down into the plain to take a "companion for me," as they expressed it, of whose approach they had had notice.

CHAPTER IX.

EXTRACT FROM MRS. MOENS'S LETTERS: MAY 17 TO JUNE 18.

Return to Naples—Hôtel de Genève—The Coppersmiths—Telegrams to England—Letter to the Brigands—Milords or Photographers—First Letter from the Hostage—A Noble Reply to a Telegram—The Second Letter—Imprisonment of the Brigand's Relatives—Arrival of H.M.S. "Magicienne"—Omniscience of the Italian Government—Sunday in Naples—Our Message stopped—The Brigandess's News—Another Letter from the Hostage—A Second Instalment prepared—Letter to the *Times*—A Visit from a supposed *Manutengulo*—I hear of a Friend coming from England—His Arrival.

CHAPTER IX.

May 17.—As soon as Mr. Aynsley rejoined us, he advised our immediate return to Naples, as he had, as I understood (in order to carry out the idea of the captive being merely a poor artist), told the brigands that he should go thither to try and raise a ransom among the English residents in that city. Our boxes were packed, and we were just ready to start, when young Mr. Bonham, the Vice-Consul, and Mr. Edward Holme,* an English resident at Naples, arrived to offer us assistance and advice.

I had the greatest disinclination to leave Salerno, as I felt that there, at all events, I was nearer to my husband, but I considered it

---

* I cannot thank this gentleman and his family too much for their kindness to my wife.—W. I. C. M.

my duty to follow Mr. Aynsley's advice, as my husband had, on parting with him, placed me under his care. On arriving at the station Mrs. Aynsley and I got into a first-class carriage, and our kind friends Mr. and Mrs. S—— joined us; but Mr. Aynsley thought that, as we should probably be followed by spies of the brigands, and our minutest actions commented on, it would be better for us to go into a second-class carriage, in order that we might not appear wives of "Milords." He thought that if they could by any means be persuaded that we were poor, they would lower their exorbitant demands. The train was on the point of starting when the guard came up and told us that a telegram had just been received to the effect that my husband was free, and that the guard at Eboli had seen him. We made further inquiries, but the additional details thrown in made us doubt the news, so we decided not to change our plans, and went on direct to Naples.

Oh, how wretched I felt when I found myself alone at the Hôtel de Genève, in the noisiest part of noisy Naples! We had been advised to go to that hotel when we came over from Sicily, as it was built on high ground, and was considered far healthier than the hotels along the Chiaja, where there had been recently many cases of fever. It is a large building in the centre of the Strada Medina, one of the great thoroughfares of Naples, and free from all the bad smells which make some parts of the town quite unendurable; but the noise is distracting. Nearly all the shops around it belong to coppersmiths, whose incessant hammering is added to the ceaseless roll of carriages and cracking of whips. Often I can scarcely hear myself speak; my only quiet hour is at twelve o'clock, when the inhabitants take their siesta. I find myself constantly repeating a text which a friend quoted to me "Alexander, the coppersmith, did me much harm."

But my great misery makes me forget all these minor worries, which I must endure patiently, for to take larger or more fashionable apartments would be inconsistent with the character which Mr. Aynsley still thinks we may be able to keep up. I was very ill when we arrived, and went directly to my room. Telegrams were immediately despatched *in my name, but without my knowledge,* to Lord Palmerston, to members of my family, and to personal friends of my husband's in London.

This is a copy of one or two of the telegrams:—

"My husband, Mr. Moens, captured by brigands, near Pæstum; 8500*l.* demanded for ransom, or life threatened.—May 18th."

"Don't be alarmed about me; am with friends. Husband taken by brigands near Pæstum: 8500 pounds ransom asked; life threatened. Can collect no money here. Urge English Government. Italian police and authorities might obtain husband's release, if properly pressed. Military useless."

The soldiers will never effect the release of my husband. You cannot imagine the difficulties of the country; 6000 troops are out, but the brigands laugh at them. To give you an idea of the audacity of the band, they positively came down from the mountains close to Prestum yesterday, and took away all the clothes of the ferrymen of the river Sele. Mr. Aynsley has sent a letter to the brigands, offering a small ransom, and telling them that that is all the money he can raise. The brigands are not yet certain whether their captives are rich "milords" or photographers. The Italian papers say two poor artists have been mistaken by the brigands for rich English lords.

May 20.—It is now five days since I saw my husband. I cannot realize my situation: I feel as if I were in some horrible dream, or rather in the Inferno. I am sure they may well say of us when we return to England, what the Florentines said of Dante: "That's the man who has been with the brigands, and that's the wife who has been in the Inferno!" My mind is harassed with perpetual false reports; but we can hear nothing certain of poor W.'s actual position. Mr. Aynsley has sent a letter for the brigands by post to a landed proprietor living at Battipaglia, whose brother was captured the same day as my husband by another band of brigands.* I believe the brigands arranged with Mr. Aynsley that all letters should be sent to this house, and that they would send messengers there for them.

In this letter Mr. Aynsley writes as a poor man, who has got up a small subscription amongst the English at Naples. He thinks the brigands

* After waiting nearly a week in the greatest anxiety, we discovered that the person to whose house the letter was directed refused to take it in; his brother having escaped, he declined holding any communication with the brigands.

will believe this letter, as when he was with them they certainly had begun to doubt whether they had got the rich prize they expected. Fortunately, when captured, Mr. Aynsley had on a very old coat of yellow silk, which he was wearing for the sake of coolness; and W.'s fingers were all stained with the chemicals he had been using when photographing. One of the brigands asked Mr. Aynsley whether his coat had been torn in the night; and was told that it had been reduced to that state from constant wear.

I have but one consolation, that we have not brought this misfortune on ourselves by any want of caution. We made every possible inquiry as to the safety of the road, and all informed us that it was quite safe, and well guarded by soldiers; in fact, numerous parties had visited the ruins every day during the past week and throughout the season. I hear a rumour that our party was mistaken for Lord Pembroke's; it is even said that the brigands had received a telegram from Rome, to be on the watch for him, as he was expected at Pæstum the very day that my husband was taken.* I feel that this would never have occurred, if the Prefect had been doing his duty. Italians are constantly being carried off to the mountains by the brigands, and the Government leaves them quietly to their fate. I am convinced that if a different plan were pursued, and the ransom levied on the province where the outrage took place, brigandage would soon be at an end.

May 21.—I was just retiring last night at eleven o'clock, when the Consul's servant arrived with a letter to me from my husband—the letter I had been so anxiously expecting, but which, when, it came made me feel that all indeed was real, and that I was cruelly separated from him, with a terrible uncertainty as to when we should meet again. A paragraph is going the

* We heard that his party visited Pæstum on the 13th.

round of the papers, that I am out of my mind from grief and anxiety. I think I should be, were it not for my sure belief in God's promise to help the weak. I keep repeating to myself that it is "He who looseth the prisoner out of captivity." The letter was dated the 19th of May, and ran as follows:—

"I am pretty well, only tired by night marches over a frightful country, and nearly starved, because the force follows the band. Don't be alarmed, dearest, but trust, as I do, in God, that I shall be restored safe to you. Telegraph to England for money, and make as good a bargain as you can. Pray for me, as I do for your peace of mind.—I am still pretty well. *Pray send all the money you can get.* The new address —'Care of Signor Elia Visconti, Commune di Giffone, Valle Piano, near Salerno.' Write immediately. One of the family of Visconti is my unfortunate companion. They are jealous of what I write. I do feel for you so, dearest; but trust in God. Telegraph for money, for I cannot stand this awful life, and long night marches. *Do not say anything to anyone except Mr. Aynsley.* They think the Government will pay for me, so I shall not get off cheap. Remember me to Mr. Aynsley, and tell him that I feel thankful that he has escaped what I have gone through."*

You will observe that he says, " Say nothing to anyone but Mr. Aynsley." But this caution came too late, the telegrams having already been sent; and the whole affair became too notorious for us to carry out the private method of arrangement which the Italians take care to adopt when any of their relatives are captured.

A member of the banking firm of Cumming, Wood, and Co., has just been to tell me that he has a credit for me for the full amount of the ransom demanded, viz., 8500*l*. This is the doing of W. S——, who has replied to Mr.

* These first letters were written in English.—W. I. C. M.

Aynsley's telegram by making himself responsible for the whole sum, advancing it at once at his own sole risk, lest delay might prove fatal to my husband. How few do we meet who are capable of such noble and generous actions as this! I have written to those who know about my husband's affairs, in hopes that some of his investments may be realized, and the proceeds handed over to my kind and generous relative—to relieve him at once from our half of the burden.

Hôtel de Genère, May 30.—The heat is now intense. I never go out until the evening, and then some kind friends come and take me for a walk. We pass down the Toledo and Chiaja to the Villa Reale. The streets are crowded with people, and stiflingly close and hot. I weep as I walk, and think over past happiness. "*Nessun maggior dolore di che ricordarsi del tempo felice nella miseria.*" How few in that gay scene imagined there was one among them suffering as I was!

The next letter I received from my husband was dated the 26th of May, and was all written in Italian:—

"I have already written to you to implore you to send the money at once. The captain of the band says he will have 50,000 ducats immediately (8500*l*.). He says, that if that sum is not sent directly, my life is lost. He will cut off my head, and send it to you without pity. I am pretty well at present; but this life in the mountains is truly insupportable and terrible, particularly now, because we are followed by the troops in great numbers, and this places my life in great danger. I am dying of hunger and fatigue, despair and continual anguish: thinking of you is my greatest grief. The captain will make me write in Italian, in which language you must reply to me, so that he may read our letters. Send the money in an iron box—as quickly as possible, and as much as possible at once. Write to England immediately to obtain money: write

to me directly, I entreat you. The place where
the money and letters are to be sent is to the
house of my unfortunate fellow-prisoner's father.
Address, 'To the Band, care of Signor Elia
Visconti, Giffone, Valle Piano, near Salerno.'
The letter must be sent by hand, *not by the
post*.

"I entreat you to send the money directly. Try
all the means possible. Go to all my country-
people, to the English consul, and the Italian Government, if possible, and also entreat that the
troops be withdrawn at once. It is impossible to
live in these horrible forests, amid perpetual rain.
I am always wet, and my clothes are not half
warm enough. Write to —— [Here followed
the names of three of his friends.] Send to
all these. Make every effort to get me out
of this horrible prison. Have faith in God,
as I have. I do not know where to direct
this letter to you. It is impossible to free
me without money. Send the money in gold.

Adieu, my dearest wife. Arrange so that the
money is sent out without the knowledge of the
authorities, or it will be very hard for me. The
captain will kill me. Send the money secretly,
and let me know the sum you send. Once more,
adieu, my dearest Annie. Up to this time I
have had no letter from you; this makes me
truly unhappy.

"Your unhappy Husband,

"W. I. C. M."*

June 3.—My husband's letters make me distracted when I think of them. God help us
both! I cry day and night unto Him.

May 31.—Mr. Aynsley has sent a letter to the
brigands to say 400*l.* would be sent to them; but
has received no answer. Two or three messengers
have been sent—one of them brother to the captain of the band. He is considered an honest cha-

* The greater part of this was dictated by the captain.

racter, and is employed on the railway. He has a safe conduct and pass from the general, which had been procured with great difficulty; but up to this time no messenger has returned. Martial law has been established all over the province, and the families of the brigands have been thrown into prison, in all, nearly 800 persons.

The brigands now have an idea that my husband is a relation of Lord Palmerston, on account of the telegram. They are about twelve miles from Salerno. Unfortunately, there is a report all over Naples that the Consul may draw for any sum of money, and we are in fear now the brigands will demand even more than 8000*l*. The Prefect, too, has just been removed to another district, which is unfortunate for us, for, although his successor has an excellent reputation, a change at such a crisis might be disastrous to us.

The *Magicienne* steam-frigate has arrived in

the Bay of Salerno. It seems at first sight rather ridiculous to send a man-of-war to Salerno to liberate a prisoner in the mountains, but from something Manzo said about being tired of his perilous way of life, Mr. Aynsley fancied that he might be induced to accept a small sum of money, and then, with his prisoner, take refuge on board the English ship, to be conveyed in safety out of the kingdom. It seems that years ago a young lady was captured by a band, and after every conceivable plan had been tried in vain, a similar one to this was adopted for her liberation, and an English man-of-war brought both her and her captors away in safety. So Mr. Aynsley mentioned the matter to the Consul-General, who, after communicating with the civil authorities at Florence and receiving their assent, obtained the permission of the English Government to request the English admiral at Malta to send up a ship.

The troops are scouring the country and acting with unwonted energy, so that it is extremely difficult to communicate with the band, and the laws are very stringent against paying money to the brigands; the punishment for so doing being twenty years at the galleys; besides, the money found on a messenger may be confiscated by the soldiers. You see, therefore, how this increases our difficulties. Every road to the mountains is guarded, and it is difficult to find any one who will run the risk of taking the money. The most insignificant individual is well known to the Government, and no one can go from one province to another without a pass. The birth-place, name, and parentage of every one of the brigands are fully known to the Government officials here.

June 4.—A great feast-day—the anniversary of Garibaldi's entrance into Naples. All the people are out in the streets in gala costume. My enemies, the tinmen, are quiet, but the church bells ring every ten minutes, and, unfortunately, the parish church is close to the hotel, and its bells are very numerous and large, and particularly loud. I was so glad when it was time for our English service, and I drove through the crowded streets, swarming with men and soldiers, to the English Church, an extremely pretty building, but very badly ventilated. In the middle of the service the heat made me feel so faint that I left Mrs. Aynsley, and went out and got into a carriage. On my way to the hotel, my carriage was stopped by the procession of soldiers. I had to wait in the burning sun while regiment after regiment of cavalry and infantry passed me. General Türr was in a carriage with his aides-de-camp. I did not enjoy the scene. The music, the gay dresses, the military pomp, only made me feel sad. I thought how differently I should have felt had my husband been with me. The sight of the soldiers to me was fearful. I always felt as if my husband was in battle, and who could tell how it might terminate? I reached my hotel at last, and shut the windows to keep out all sound. How desolate and wretched I was! What gnawing anxiety at my heart! How I longed for one of my sisters to be with me, it is so very hard to bear grief alone! St. Paul knew well this craving of the human heart when he said, "Bear ye one another's burdens."

(There is one lesson I hope I have learnt through this heavy trial, and that is, to seek out the wretched—not to wait for the wretched to seek me—and to try and comfort them by cheerful and consoling words: to give them a little of my time. Many want that more than money, which can never make up for want of sympathy.)

In the evening there were splendid illuminations in honour of Garibaldi.

I was so wretched at this hotel that I longed to go elsewhere, but Mr. and Mrs. Aynsley persuaded me to try the fourth story, as they still thought of keeping up the character which they hoped the brigands believed to belong to Mr. Aynsley and my husband. I always felt convinced that it would be impossible to deceive the brigands, still I thought it better to acquiesce; and in accordance with their suggestions, I received no visits from my countrywomen. Those who know how ready English people are to sympathize with their compatriots in trouble in a foreign land, can easily imagine of how much comfort and sympathy I was thus depriving myself!

I accordingly went up higher, where I had a large room, and my experience of Italian hotels teaches me always to choose either the third or fourth stories, where one avoids the bad smells, and the air is fresher. I had a fine view of Vesuvius from my room. The volcano was somewhat active during the whole of my stay. I am anxiously expecting news from Salerno, as Manzo's brother has not yet returned.

June 6.—After a week of the utmost anxiety, expecting every hour the return of the messenger (Manzo's brother), his mother has come to us in great distress, to tell us that he is in prison heavily ironed—he was provided with a pass signed by General Balegno, the head of the forces in the province of Salerno, and countersigned by our Consul-General, Mr. Bonham; but notwithstanding, he was stopped by a captain of Carbineers, who, on his own responsibility, arrested him, and without informing us of what had happened, has kept him prisoner, until he had further instructions from his commanding officer; of course Mr. Bonham will soon procure his release, but this delay is terrible: what must it be to my poor husband!

The Consul is acting with great care: both he and all his advisers are afraid that if they were to give the whole amount at once, the brigands would not be satisfied, but require just as much again—this is the idea and fear of every one.

A brigandess has given herself up to the authorities. She was shot in the arm, through some carelessness on the part of one of the band. For seven days she remained with the brigands; though the arm was fractured, the brigands would not let her leave them: at last she was so ill, she got away and came to Salerno, and presented herself to the authorities; her arm was then amputated. She had so much nerve that she refused chloroform, and neither groaned nor complained. The only sign she gave of suffering was clenching her teeth. When the surgeons left her she said, "Remember, I had eighteen napoleons about me when I came here; I must have them again when I am well!" She says my husband is well, and a favourite with the band, because he walks well, and gives no trouble, and amuses himself with sketching. This news is better than nothing, but still I cannot help feeling intensely anxious for him, as the troops are still in pursuit. In his letter to me, he wrote that the captain of the band says he will never give him up to the troops alive. The brigands have refused to go on board the frigate: they send word the English climate would not agree with their health; it is too cold.

The last report in Naples is that my husband and the brigands have joined together to get as much money as they possibly can, and that he intends to join the band.

The first instalment of money was at last successfully conveyed to the mountains, and on the 8th June, I received the following letter written (in Italian) on the 6th of June :—

"Write to me, I pray you. I think of you continually. I am indeed unhappy; the horrors of the life I am leading are indescribable. I am exposed to all the inclemency of the weather; I am dying of hunger, cold, wet, and anguish. I believe that you would do everything to see me again. Borrow money directly, and send it immediately to the mountains to ransom me. The captain has received the 10,000 francs that you have sent me, and he sends you word that to free me, 50,000 ducats are required. This sum, therefore, must be collected if you wish to see me again. I entreat you to borrow of ————, or of ————, the remainder to make up the 50,000 ducats, and send the money to Visconti's house. Do not hope to liberate me for a less sum. Here I am in constant peril. I cannot possibly remain much longer in good health. I send you, by Signor Visconti, a little gift, cut by my own hand: prize it, and think often of me. Send the things that I have written for, and send immediately. Adieu, dearest; pray write to me, and believe in my sufferings and in my affections. Have faith in God.

"Your affectionate husband,

"W. J. C. M.

"The bands treat me very badly: I cannot endure it.

" P.S.—I pray you to get the troops withdrawn, if you love me. The captain says that I may be liberated by the troops, but I shall not be alive. He also says that the money, 10,000 francs, is not enough to buy bread for me."

This letter was sent to Signor Visconti, at Giffone, and by him forwarded to me through the Consul-General.

Immediately on receipt of it we took measures for forwarding a further sum to the brigands, and we determined on limiting the next instalment to 17,000 francs, in the hope that the robbers would let my husband go on receipt of that sum without demanding more.

Signor Visconti, whose son had been for three weeks my husband's companion in captivity, has paid me a visit of condolence, accompanied by his son.

June 13.—I sent my letter to the *Times*, not

having seen Mr. Aynsley's letter, because every one keeps writing to me from England that life with the brigands cannot be so very unpleasant after all, and this too at the time when I am receiving such dreadful letters from my husband. I was determined that the real state of the case should be known, and yet I was frightened at my own boldness in "writing to the *Times*," and actually carried the letter to and fro between the hotel and the post-office several times before I could summon up courage to post it.

I am still in fearful suspense and anxiety. We are now negotiating through Signor Visconti, who is a rich landed proprietor at Giffone, fourteen miles from Salerno. He has been forced by the brigands themselves to receive our money and letters. His son and nephew have been with the brigands two months, and he has had to pay 4150*l.* ransom for the two.

A gentleman who is believed to be connected with the brigands* came yesterday to see me, on purpose to find out if we were very rich people. I was warned of his coming, and prepared accordingly. I had many lectures given me to appear bold and indifferent, so that the brigands might not extort much through my fears. I fortunately wore my hat, which concealed the tears which constantly came into my eyes. He told us he had heard there was an enormous sum waiting to be used as ransom, and that the brigands believed my husband to be a nobleman, and that the Government would pay. So you see the difficulties we have to contend with, not to mention the distance the brigands are off. It takes such a very long time to do anything. It is indeed trying, I feel it sometimes unbearable.

If the troops do not prevent us, the consul-general sends to-morrow some more money,

* I need scarcely say that we do not now believe in this connexion.

some flannels, a water-proof coat, and a Bible.
My husband has written to me for these
things. He seems to suffer so from cold—
very different from us at Naples, who are melt-
ing with the heat. He sent me a little wooden
cross, which he had amused himself in carving.
His letters are all in Italian, as before. The life
must be terrible for him. I only hope and pray
some one is coming to me from England, for I
am in a very lonely position.

June 17—There was a very fearful storm last
night. It began in the evening, and lasted until
one or two o'clock in the morning. I could not
rest, thinking of my husband being exposed to
its violence, with no shelter.

At this time H. C., one of my brothers-in-law,
was on his way to Naples to see what he could
do for us. I afterwards heard that he went to
Florence *en route*, and was very kindly received
there by the British envoy, who introduced him
to some of the ministers, and procured from them

for him letters of introduction and recommendation to the principal local authorities (civil and military) at Salerno. These letters were of the greatest possible use in furthering the requests which he afterwards preferred to these important officials personally on the spot, accompanied by the consul-general or Mr. Richard Holme.

On the 17th June, a gentleman who had travelled with H. C. from Genoa to Leghorn, called on me at his request to let me know that my friend was close at hand. It was a great satisfaction to me to hear that I should so soon have the assistance of one whom I knew well.

On the 18th of June Mr. C—— appeared at the Hôtel de Genève at breakfast. I was so delighted to see him. Only those who have been so long in trouble amongst strangers, and separated from their own kith and kin, can understand the pleasure with which I now found near me the husband of a sister. We talked of my old home, and of the kind hearts that felt for me there. Really sometimes it seemed almost worth while to be placed in my present unhappy position just to learn what truly good, and kind, and loving hearts there are in the world. And in the fresh wonder and excitement of hearing what my friends at home had done and said about me, I for a moment forgot my great sorrow. But time was precious, and my newly arrived friend lost not a moment in seeking out the consul-general, and deliberating with him and Mr. Aynsley on what was to be done for my husband.

END OF THE FIRST VOLUME.

www.ingramcontent.com/pod-product-compliance
Lightning Source LLC
Chambersburg PA
CBHW030730230426
43667CB00007B/659